The Saddest Thing Is That I Have Had to Use Words

The Saddest Thing Is
That I Have Had to Use Words:
A Madeline Gins Reader

edited by Lucy Ives

siglio

2020

siglio uncommon books at the intersection of art & literature

PO BOX 111, Catskill, New York 12414 Tel: 310-857-6935 www.sigliopress.com

Available to the trade through D.A.P./Artbook.com
75 Broad Street, Suite 630, New York, NY 10004
Tel: 212-627-1999 Fax: 212-627-9484

Table of Contents

WORD RAIN
(or A Discursive Introduction
to the Intimate Philosophical Investigations
of G,R,E,T,A, G,A,R,B,O, It Says)
78

Selections from *What the President Will Say and Do!!*

Selections from *Helen Keller or Arakawa*

Remember if you are not sick,* there is no cure for you.

As for everything going wrong, having gone wrong, it has been only a matter of time.

These are things with which things go wrong.

Is or was the world a cure? Or is there a cure outside the world?

*If you are sick, you are lucky because you might have/win a cure.

—Madeline Gins

EVERYTHING I RECEIVE WILL BECOME PART OF
A NOVEL: An Introduction to the Work of Madeline Gins

LUCY IVES

I have thought for a while about where to begin. The writer, artist, and architect Madeline Gins (1941–2014) did so much during her lifetime—in spheres literary, philosophical, visual, and environmental, and in between—that to begin at any single beginning feels disingenuous if not downright incorrect. To depart from a solitary point would be to miss or minimize all the many beginnings Gins began, the new paths of research, the collaborations, the explorations of new disciplines, media, forms. So I won't simply say that Madeline Gins was born in New York City in the midst of the Second World War and raised on Long Island, in the village of Island Park; that she went on to study Eastern philosophy and physics at Barnard; that in the early 1960s, while studying painting at the Brooklyn Museum Art School, she met, collaborated with, and, in 1965, married Nagoya-born artist Shūsaku Arakawa; that she is perhaps best known, as of the writing of this introduction, for her work with Arakawa on the Reversible Destiny architectural project, via which they designed and oversaw the realization of structures they believed had the capacity to stave off death, including lofts in Tokyo, a park in Yoro, Japan, and a house in East Hampton. All this is true, but I want to begin not with a beginning but in the early middle of things, in a social world that was also a world of work and art.

It is the spring of 1969. Kurt Vonnegut's grand novel of military-industrial historical trauma *Slaughterhouse-Five* has appeared in March (*The Godfather* and *I Know Why the Caged Bird Sings* also enter the world this year), and later this summer the Stonewall Uprising will take place, two Americans will walk on the moon, Charles Manson's "family" will commit their notorious killings, and the murder of Meredith Hunter at the Rolling Stones' Altamont Free Concert will signal the coming devolution of hippie culture (often into consumer lifestyle). The West Coast of the United States is the crucible of globally disseminated psychedelia and cowboy narratives. Meanwhile, back east, New York City has long since "stole[n] the idea of modern art," as Serge Guilbaut puts it, from Paris, that capital of the nineteenth century.[1] Valerie Solanas shot Andy Warhol last June, and the mega-valuation of contemporary artworks we are accustomed to today is well underway.

But it is spring. The war in Vietnam continues. A younger generation of American artists has begun to bypass the standard practices of the Manhattan gallery system in favor of discursive modes of circulation; this will shortly be understood as the shift from Abstract Expressionism and other later-modernist object-based artistic movements to so-called conceptualism. The British-American collaborative group Art & Language is publishing its magazine *Art-Language* and American artist Joseph Kosuth argues in his essay "Art After Philosophy" that art has a privileged relationship to language. In Kosuth's view, "any physical thing" can be considered an artwork; thus, the work of art inheres in the language-based contention that a given thing is art. Art is, and is *only*, "a kind of proposition presented within the context of art as a comment on art."[2] (In 1967, Sol LeWitt laid the grounds for Kosuth's more specific contention, writing in "Paragraphs on Conceptual Art" that conceptual work is meant "to engage the mind of the viewer rather than his eye or emotions."[3]) But we need not see the trends grouped under the term conceptualism as either monolithic in nature or occurring exclusively in relation to philosophy. A broad swathe of interdisciplinary

1 See Serge Guilbaut, *How New York Stole the Idea of Modern Art: Abstract Expressionism, Freedom, and the Cold War*, trans. Arthur Goldhammer (Chicago: University of Chicago Press, 1983), in which Guilbaut traces relationships between and among the U.S. government's imperialist ambitions after the Second World War, the nation's artistic movements, criticism, and the art market.

2 Joseph Kosuth, "Art After Philosophy," in *Art in Theory 1900–1990: An Anthology of Changing Ideas*, ed. Charles Harrison and Paul Wood (London and Malden, MA: Blackwell, 2003), 856–57.

3 Sol LeWitt, "Paragraphs on Conceptual Art," in *Conceptual Art: A Critical Anthology*, ed. Alexander Alberro and Blake Stimson (Cambridge, MA: MIT Press, 1999), 15.

practitioners are at work in spring of '69. Vito Acconci, a poet and artist, and poet Bernadette Mayer have convened a series of events they are calling "Street Works," the results and documentation of which they will publish as a supplement to their magazine of experimental writing, *0 TO 9*, a project they've been jointly pursuing for the past two years.

Among the artists bringing language off the page and into the busy thoroughfares of Manhattan in the three collaborative "Street Works" happenings—March 15th, April 18th, and May 25th—is poet-novelist Madeline Gins. She is in her late twenties, the wife of an up-and-coming mentee of Marcel Duchamp, who, along with his mentor, has recently exhibited work in the Dwan Gallery's remarkable 1967 show, "Language to Be Looked at and/or Things to Be Read." This artist, who now goes by a single moniker, Arakawa, also joins, bringing with him a large plastic sheet depicting the floor plan of a house, imagery that sometimes appears in his paintings.[4] The floor plan is to be spread out on the sidewalk so that passersby must cross such terms as "BEDROOM" and "BATH" to get to wherever they are going. It's witty, sweet, and a little puzzling. Gins's contribution feels more ambitious—utopian, even—if equally odd. It takes the form of a "GROUP NOVEL." She is handing out facsimiles of a typed questionnaire that instructs the reader, "EVERYTHING I RECEIVE WILL BECOME PART OF A NOVEL (MY PUBLISHER HAS EXPRESSED INTEREST IN THIS PROJECT)." She claims that all completed forms mailed back to her P.O. box at the Canal Street post office will be used in the composition of her novel and that all respondents will be credited. "IF YOU WISH TO ADD PAGES (ANYTHING) DO," she invites the anonymous addressee. She is writing to anyone and everyone and seems to mean it, although I have not been able to find any evidence of a manuscript related to this project in Gins's archive, alas. The questionnaire itself functions a bit like a Mad Lib, with blanks interrupting

4 See Gins's remarks in her essay included in this collection, "Arakawa's Painting, *Diagram of Part of the Imagination*: A Fictional Working Out of Fictions (1963–64)," in which she gives a close reading of Arakawa's use of a floor plan in one of his paintings.

Opposite + following page: Untitled by Madeline Gins, published in the *Street Works* edition of *0 TO 9*, edited by Vito Acconci and Bernadette Mayer, 1969.

PLEASE FINISH THESE SENTENCES AND RETURN THIS PAPER TO:
MADELINE GINS,P.O.BOX 299, CANAL ST. STATION,NEW YORK,
N.Y.10013. EVERYTHING I RECEIVE WILL BECOME PART OF A
NOVEL(MY PUBLISHER HAS EXPRESSED INTEREST IN THIS PROJECT)
THE LENGTH OF WHICH WILL BE DETERMINED BY THE NUMBER OF
REPLIES SENT. IF YOU WISH TO ADD PAGES(ANYTHING)PLEASE
DO,I WILL GIVE YOU CREDIT FOR ANYTHING OF YOURS I USE.THIS
IS A GROUP NOVEL, AN HISTORICAL NOVEL, AN EXPLORATION OF
THE NATURE OF CONSCIOUSNESS.

My name,_____,belongs to_____

_____. I am_____old and I have_____more years

to live. Another name for me might be_____.

As I walked down_____I was_____from my

address. In front of me,I particularly noticed_____

_____in back of me was_____on my left side

_____on the right_____.

I_____heard _____. I knew my left side

from my right by_____

_____. I was_____

_____.

I move according to_____

_____. I am composed of_____

and_____. This falls into_____parts. The

heaviest part to move is_____.

I felt my thoughts to physically be in(out)_____
                                                (Be Specific)
_____. The material of which they

are made is_____which operates_____

_____

_____. In front of these is _____in back_____

_____. I walk in_____

_____.

I_____

_____

_____.

_____ said something extraordinary:"_____

_____

(Choose a Quote)
_____
                                              ."
_____
                                              ."

Memory is_____.

"_____?" I asked.

IT'S FINE TO LEAVE BLANKS IF YOU MUST

POSSIBLE ADDITIONS AFTER THE 'FACT':

_____

_____

_____ if _____

_____

_____

_____

_____

_____

_____ but _____

_____

_____

_____

_____

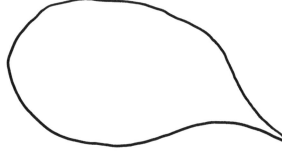

sentence-fragments, "I am_____old and I have_____more years to live." Or, "I am composed of_____and_____." The back of the form includes an empty speech bubble, presumably to be used for any final interjections, complaints, or requests.

Gins's "Street Works" contribution seems particularly significant to me because it shows Gins in the midst of imagining literature as a radically collaborative undertaking. She is, here, in some sense literalizing the suggestion implicit in Roland Barthes's essay on "The Death of the Author," published in English just two years earlier in the rarified art-world magazine *Aspen*, in its "Minimalism"-themed issue, edited by Brian O'Doherty. Barthes calls for literary writing to be understood as text, as a "tissue of citations" referring back to an unknowable number of contexts and referents, rather than as a monographic masterpiece, the meaning of which is exhaustively foreseen by a god-like author.[5] With her group novel, which she also terms "AN HISTORICAL NOVEL, AN EXPLORATION OF THE NATURE OF CONSCIOUSNESS," Gins inhabits the so-called author function, without attempting to act as the sole originator of the novel's meaning. This is profoundly synthetic and polyvocal literary production, presaging and perhaps even predicting contemporary platform-enabled, collaborative writing online.

The author's "death," whether provoked by Barthes's essay or not, was certainly palpable to artists in Anglophone and Francophone avant-gardes of the late 1960s. It invited a view of the category of literature as, 1. synthetic, and 2. collaborative, and this was a notion that would stay with Gins throughout her career. Yet, while it is important to foreground this moment and milieu as influential for Gins, I would like, with at least equal urgency, to call the reader's attention to the unique way in which, in her questionnaire, Gins imagines reading and writing as co-implicated and nearly synonymous activities. The respondent must read blanks that give a vague indication of narrative sentences. The subsequent act of filling-in is an effort of interpretation—an effort to read—as much as an effort at articulation, description, or completion, i.e., writing. Reading and writing cannot be cleanly

5 Roland Barthes, "The Death of the Author," in *Image, Music, Text*, trans. Stephen Heath (New York: Hill & Wang, 1977), 146.

separated out, cannot be understood as absolutely distinct activities or roles. Indeed, as the group novel was never actually written, it exists only as a projected novel-to-come, an infinite series of possible interpretations of the blanks present in the questionnaire. I point out this special temporality implied by Gins's questionnaire, a time irresolvably *between* the times of reading and writing, because the ambiguity it brings to our attention is distinct from the ambiguity Barthes focuses on in his famous essay, although the two are certainly related. In Gins's revision of the literary object, the author dies, not through the invalidation of all copyright, as in Barthes, but because the author, a writer, was always the reader, too. She writes, in her experimental novel, to be published in the fall of 1969, of the work of writing on behalf of a given reader, "I symbolize your existence for you as I read your life."

The full title of Gins's early masterpiece is *WORD RAIN (or A Discursive Introduction to the Intimate Philosophical Investigations of G,R,E,T,A, G,A,R,B,O, It Says)*. The book was brought forth in an elegant, now extremely rare hardcover edition by Grossman Publishers, an imprint run by the daring Richard Grossman, who in 1965 had published Ralph Nader's bestselling *Unsafe at Any Speed: The Designed-In Dangers of the American Automobile*, a detailed exploration of the U.S. automotive industry's resistance to changes in car design that would improve driver and pedestrian safety. Grossman apparently used funds from sales of books like Nader's (which, not incidentally, was followed by the passage of seatbelt laws in forty-nine states as well as the creation of the Department of Transportation) to make possible the publication of challenging material like Gins's novel. It is an unusual and lucky thing that he did: *WORD RAIN* is arguably Gins's most brilliant endeavor and among the most significant works of experimental prose of the second half of the twentieth century.

WORD RAIN is a carefully calibrated and constructed artist's book, as well as a comment on the novel form. It activates multiple registers of the reading experience, asking the reader to attend to the book's design and physical form, to the writing itself, and to the interplay between the text and various images included. The games begin at the dust jacket, which shows a photograph of a hardcover book ostensibly identical to the

WORD RAIN the reader holds in their hands, save that this *WORD RAIN*'s cover is blank. This truncated *mise en abyme* suggests that *WORD RAIN* contains an image of itself, with a difference, in that the reader must supply the subsequent image that this image of the book (this imaginary book) will contain. Without the reader's participation—what Barthes called "the birth of the reader"—*WORD RAIN*'s meaning is incomplete.[6] This indeterminacy is far from accidental; it constitutes a strategic displacement of the reader from the position of guileless identification sometimes associated with the first-person address of lyric poetry or the protagonist of hero narratives or the *Bildungsroman*. *WORD RAIN* compels the reader to acknowledge the mediating objects that are printed words, the page, and the book, as well as the reader's own role in the fabrication of fictional events.

But all this sounds rather dry, and *WORD RAIN* is far from dry. On several pages, a photograph of a hirsute thumb appears, reminding us that the reader's (apparently male) presence has been foreseen and already exists as a part of the book's fiction. As the dutiful jacket copy of the first edition proclaims, in what is perhaps the understatement of 1969, "In recreating the imaginative act of reading, Madeline Gins has written a very unusual book." The copy also attempts to summarize this "very unusual" novel's plot, describing a scenario of simultaneously minor and significant events:

> In *WORD RAIN*, an unnamed narrator sits at a desk in a friend's apartment reading a manuscript. Surrounding the undefined character is a birthday party taking place in the next room, a glass of pineapple-grapefruit juice that is supposed to be pure grapefruit juice, the loose leaves of the manuscript, and the variable weather conditions. The pages of the manuscript slide to the floor. The weather turns misty and cold. Dishes rattle in the kitchen nearby. A package is delivered. It feels like rain. As each of these distractions occur playing against themselves [sic] in almost musical variation, the reader either opposes or flows with them as she reads. Sitting at the desk, she sometimes skims pages

6 Barthes, 148.

The Saddest Thing Is That I Have Had to Use Words   17

day-dreaming or catches the rhythms and reads in word blocks while the text fills itself in with the surrounding noises, conversations and entrances of the people in the apartment—rain at the window punctuates the words as her attention drifts to the weather, a dish breaking in the kitchen drains the impact of a melodramatic moment in the manuscript.

Yet this mild and attractive précis, likely the work of a publicist or Grossman himself, is only loosely accurate. The reader of *WORD RAIN* will find numerous other textual strategies: citations and appropriations of material from other books, the use of an eccentric form of mathematical notation (what Gins calls "oiled geometry, liniment algebra and creamed mathematics") to quantify the text, as well as a detailed accounting of the painful, exciting, banal phenomenology of reading.[7] The narrator's reading has peculiar results—special effects, one might say. At times she seems to encounter a version of herself in the text, whom she attempts to instruct or salute as from a great distance; these moments feel elegiac, suggesting that reading can be an act of reconciliation with, or loss of, the self. At other times, the effects felt by the protagonist-reader are directly physical, synesthetic, as in a passage in which words ossify, "The word face was a stone. The word guess was a flint. The words a, the, in, by, up, it, were pebbles. The word laughter was marble. Run was cartilage." Eventually, at the end of this passage, the protagonist-reader seems to become one with these textured, surfaced words, "The word read was mica

7 As the colophon of the original edition of *WORD RAIN* states, Gins included quotations from works by Joseph Conrad, Luisa May Alcott, Alain Robbe-Grillet, Samuel Beckett, Georges Simenon, Virginia Woolf, Murasaki Shikibu, Fyodor Dostoyevsky, Thomas Hardy, Herman Melville, Jean-Paul Sartre, Jonathan Swift, Gertrude Stein, Vladimir Nabokov, James Joyce, and Edith Wharton.

Gins's imaginary math in her novel may remind one of the imaginary math devised by the artist Hanne Darboven (1941–2009), whom Gins may have encountered in New York in the late 1960s. Darboven's math permitted a "valuation" of dates by means of which all the figures used in a given date were summed to produce a new value, or *Konstruktion*. Darboven's math resembled accounting, perhaps a reference to her family's coffee business. Gins's math is designed to account for the number of words and letters used in a page; it allows for an alternate method of representing a page of writing, i.e., by means other than semantic paraphrase, and therefore seems related to Gins's understanding of writing and reading as having quantifiable, material qualities.

BUTTER

Boom in boom in, butter. Leave a grain and show it, show it. I spy.

It is a need it is a need that a flower a state flower. It is a need that a state rubber. It is a need that a state rubber is sweet and sight and a swelled stretch. It is a need. It is a need that state rubber.

Wood a supply. Clean little keep a strange, estrange on it.

Make a little white, no and not with pit, pit on in within.

END OF SUMMER

Little eyelets that have hammer and a check with stripes between a lounge, in wit, in a rested development.

SAUSAGES

Sausages in between a glass.

There is read butter. A loaf of it is managed. Wake a question. Eat an instant, answer.

A reason for bed is this, that a decline, any decline is poison, poison is a toe a toe extractor, this means a solemn change. Hanging.

No evil is wide, any extra in leaf is so strange and singular a red breast.

CELERY

Celery tastes tastes where in curled lashes and little bits and mostly in remains.

A green acre is so selfish and so pure and so enlivened.

Above: Selection from *Tender Buttons* by Gertrude Stein, 1914. This work is in the public domain.

and I was granite," a phrase in which the "I" mentioned is at once a word in the fictional manuscript the protagonist reads and also a possible name for the reader, herself. In either case—in either reading—reading is transporting, alchemical, uncontrollable. Gins's fictional account of reading erodes categories of all kinds.

But this is only to begin to think through *WORD RAIN*'s flourishes and switches at the level of letters, words, sentences; *WORD RAIN* is also remarkable for the way in which it carries on a longer (and largely unidentified) literary tradition focusing on the interaction of the human sensorium with the tactile, durational object that is the codex. Although I have so far invited comparison to Barthes's account of the author under erasure, I think parallels exist between Gins's first novel and high modernist interventions such as Gertrude Stein's *Tender Buttons* and Max Ernst's early Surrealist collage novels. As the late scholar Ulla E. Dydo has shown, *Tender Buttons* is not just or merely, as some have argued, a "Cubist" take on domestic space and the familiar words that describe and inhabit it. Rather, it is a lexicon of an actual intimate language, a love code shared by Stein and her partner, Alice B. Toklas.[8] Similarly, Ernst's reconfigurations of Victorian imagery suggest a highly personal dreamscape, by turns erotic and alarming. These early twentieth-century works (*Tender Buttons* dates from 1914 and Ernst began his collages around 1922) are often treated as doctrinal examples of Modernist and Surrealist poetics, with emphatically capitalized "m" and "s." Yet, they are far more compelling for the unique sensual languages to which they give the reader access than for their critiques of bourgeois institutions, or, for that matter, their participation in influential movements. Perhaps nothing could be more obvious. However, it seems important to emphasize the way in which these artists made use of embodied experience as a basis for intervention into the book form; similarly, *WORD RAIN* documents the event of being human in proximity to a book, as well as to the category, "book." We might think, too, here, of the eccentrically exhaustive realism of Romanian-Swiss artist Daniel Spoerri, whose *An Anecdoted Typography of Chance*, published in French in 1962 and in English in 1966, maps and describes

8 See Ulla E. Dydo, *Gertrude Stein: The Language that Rises*, 1923–1934 (Northwestern University Press: Evanston, IL, 2003).

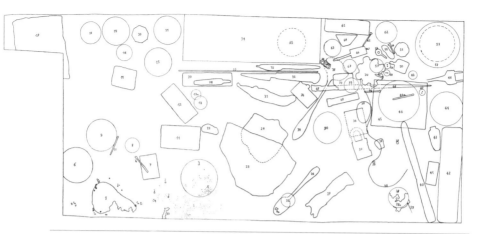

Above: "Cubist View of My Room, No 13, Hotel Carcassone," the frontispiece from *An Anecdoted Topography of Chance* by Daniel Spoerri, edited by Emmett Williams, published by Something Else Press, 1966. With permission of Daniel Spoerri.

everyday objects on a table in extensive detail—offering a sort of "voyage around my table," to paraphrase the title of Xavier de Maistre's 1794 account of his bedroom, *Voyage autour de ma chamber* (Voyage Around My Room), composed while the writer was under house arrest. Indeed, if we peer for a moment into the mid-eighteenth century, a comparison to Laurence Sterne's travesty of the picaresque novel *The Life and Opinions of Tristram Shandy, Gentleman*, with its numerous narrative digressions and famous inked-out page, seems apropos, as well. Much like these multiple forebears, *WORD RAIN* simultaneously reimagines the novel's appearance (its typographic and visual form) and its discursive structures, along with the very space and time of everyday life.

Regarding his 1968 novel *Nombres* (Numbers), among his other early revolutionary works, the French fiction writer and critic Philippe Sollers has maintained that he writes in opposition to the novel as a "subject for polite conversation," discarding from the outset any notion of literary voice (i.e., narration) as unified, controlled, or ultimately controllable.[9] Gins seems to have set out in similar opposition to the novel as a mere entertainment. However,

9 Phillipe Sollers, *Writing and the Experience of Limits*, ed. David Hayman, trans. Philip Barnard and Hayman (New York: Columbia UP, 1983), 185.

I can't speculate about what caused Gins to feel as strongly as she did that proximity to literary objects results in a sort of explosion of consciousness along multiple lines of thought and physical sensation, with all the detail of the weather as described by Dorothy Wordsworth; why it is that, as Gins writes in *WORD RAIN*, "Every book fell through me," or, as this paragraph continues, why she feels herself dispersed, in and by language: "The way bubbles are held in soapy water, conversation is held in me, and when I blow, it is vocalized. I travel in words." Gins has inverted the English Romantic poet John Keats's celebrated negative capability, in which "not myself goes home to myself": In Gins's conception of the poetic act, her subjectivity is already myriad and in outward motion, traveling, networked, reflecting and reflected, but also interrupted, even violently mediated by bookish things.[10] Gins at one time created a book-cover mockup, perhaps intended for *WORD RAIN*, that literalizes this situation. It shows a photograph of the author, seen in profile from above, with a small book like a headband splitting her skull, a trickle of blood oozing out. This subject would seem to have reading on the brain.

A theme of interruption of the human organism by literature and philosophy, perhaps by Western culture writ large, perhaps by language itself, is also present in the work of two other artists who participated in the 1969 "Street Works" happenings, Adrian Piper and Hannah Weiner. Weiner was a friend of Gins's, the author of clairvoyant poetry produced through the transcription of words she claimed appeared to her on various surfaces, including other people's faces, as well as poems appropriating maritime code. Weiner was concerned with communication across vast distances, how, as she wrote in an essay published in summer of 1969 in *0 TO 9*, people would "deal with" the overwhelming quantities of information postwar society was generating.[11] She explored the effects of the new ubiquity of communication technologies, recording devices, and data on physical gesture and interpersonal space in her

10 Keats's letter was written on October 27th, 1818, to Richard Woodhouse. See John Keats, *The Letters of John Keats: 1814–1821, Volume I*, ed. Hyder Rollins (Cambridge, U.K., and New York: Cambridge UP, 1958), 386–87.

11 Hannah Weiner, "Trans-Space Communication," *0 TO 9*, vol. 6 (July 1969): 100. See also Patrick Durgin's excellent *Hannah Weiner's Open House* (Berkeley, CA: Kenning Editions, 2007).

Above: Untitled work by Madeline Gins. Date unknown. From the Reversible Destiny Foundation Archives.

Above: Adrian Piper, *Food for the Spirit*, 1971. 14 silver gelatin prints (photographic reprints 1997). 14.95" x 14.56". Details, left to right, top to bottom: #1, #2, #7, #8, #12, #14. Collection of the Museum of Modern Art, New York © Adrian Piper Research Archive Foundation Berlin.

writing and performances. Piper, meanwhile, was just embarking on a career as an analytic philosopher in the late 1960s and early 1970s, and in 1971 created a series of photographs titled *Food for the Spirit*, which documents her experience reading Immanuel Kant's *Critique of Pure Reason*, while fasting and practicing yoga in isolation in her downtown loft. Kant's view of cognition's relationship to categories, deeply and even performatively apprehended through Piper's practice during this time, threatened to displace Piper's sense of self and being. The photographs, made in various states of undress before a mirror, brought the artist back to the immediate presence of her body and, thus, her self, in the midst of her engagement with the magnum opus of one of Western modernity's most influential authors.

Gins, like Piper and Weiner, was exploring states of extreme influence, even possession, by literary language. Her way of "deal[ing] with" the displacement of her self by an influx of words was to write in the very space of delay and estrangement that reading and writing produce, to continue this delay, this interruption. She seemed truly not to aspire to any sort of fixed meaning—or, rather, to aspire to *unfixing* meaning—even as she was quite insistent that she wrote in the novel form. Marshall McLuhan's catch phrase (*Understanding Media* had appeared in 1964) might be inverted to useful effect where *WORD RAIN* is concerned. *The message is the medium*; in other words, the message is not purely or even *actually* semantic, "It comes with a room, light, a country, sky and weather," as Gins writes of sentences encountered by *WORD RAIN*'s protagonist-reader. Given the ubiquity of computing in our own time, in the time in which I am writing this introduction, I think it is easier for a contemporary reader to grasp Gins's relationship to writing, to script, as process. I see Gins's composition in *WORD RAIN* as fundamentally cybernetic. As scholar Orit Halpern writes, "In cybernetic understandings, descriptions of processes always become sites for further production of new techniques of production rather than static descriptions; materiality, action, and concept are inseparable."[12] Whereas modernist poetries tend to understand words as having thing-like qualities, Gins is engaged in imagining a message/word that behaves like a platform, receiver, or trampoline

12 Orit Halpern, *Beautiful Data: A History of Vision and Reason Since 1945* (Durham, NC: Duke UP, 2015), 57.

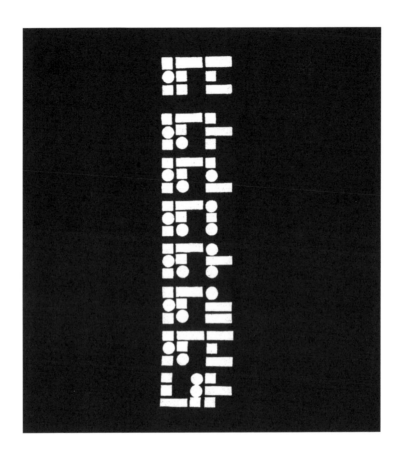

CHW	Pirates
CJD	I was plundered by a pirate
CJF	Describe the pirate
CJN	She is armed
CJP	How is she armed?
CJS	She has long guns
CJW	I have no long guns
BLD	I am a complete wreck

Above: "Pirates" from *Code Poems* by Hannah Weiner, published by Open Book Publications, a division of Station Hill Press, 1982. With permission of Charles Bernstein for Hannah Weiner in trust.

(all terms hers), a message that is in fact a medium, a conduit unstilled. Although it is, in some sense, sad to have to use words at all (and, in so doing, to delay the careening fluidity of sense), the act of reconfiguring the messaging capacity of words via "intimate philosophical investigations," as *WORD RAIN*'s subtitle goes, offers more to the reader by way of agency than it ultimately disables, confines, or withholds. "The saddest thing is that I have had to use words," Gins writes, as the titular "G,R,E,T,A, G,A,R,B,O." The strange spelling of this pseudonym (a reference to the infamously melancholic star of Hollywood's Golden Age) also indicates an acrostic set of "platforms," as Gins notes in the novel's third chapter. "G" is not merely a letter but, in Gins's eccentric formulation, also indicates "grate or gas," much as "E" is "energy," and so on. These letters lead us not into meaning but into unstable materiality and process. Gins's cybernetics is not instrumental, nor is her sadness lyrical. Rather, the melancholy of G,R,E,T,A, G,A,R,B,O is "substantially insubstantial"; it is a description of a process, giving rise to further processes; a leave-taking and a gift—a sort of visionary cybernetics.

> You may look at everything. You will see only what I see. Look at this sentence. There is nothing on it. Now look at this sentence. I see a plate of desert ribbed with dunes held in place with drops of slime just above a layer of petrified tentacles. There is nothing in this sentence. I say I see a book in this sentence. Without me, it words the page; yet says nothing.
> Words.

But this collection does not begin with *WORD RAIN*. Gins was a writer long before this early masterpiece and she would continue to be one after it. *The Saddest Thing Is That I Have Had to Use Words: A Madeline Gins Reader* begins, instead, with the loosely dated poems from the 1960s and '70s I first read in Gins's archive. I began my research in this archive in early 2017, making visits on a regular basis.

An aside here to explain my own interest: This began at some point in 2003 or '04, when I was a student at the Iowa Writers' Workshop. I was wandering around Prairie Lights, Iowa City's excellent bookstore, killing time before a reading (I was painfully shy and smartphones had not yet been invented). I was in the art book section, then on the second floor, near the windows (I do not know if it is there now). Here I happened upon a thick hardcover catalogue from Arakawa + Gins's 1997 exhibition at the Guggenheim Museum, devoted to their collaboration on Reversible Destiny. I had grown up in New York and had a vague memory of the show. Moreover, the book seemed different, promising, definitely strange. The materials it contained would not resolve themselves into a style of image I felt that I had seen before. The book was expensive, nearly $60 as I recall, a fortune in a town where $1 pints were not unusual. I did not buy it but walked down to the university library the next day, where I learned that Madeline Gins was also a writer. The University of Iowa is unusual in possessing a copy of *WORD RAIN* and not only this: It is sitting out in the stacks, not sequestered in a rare-book collection. You can find it there today. You can also find a copy of my master's thesis, a set of poems I put together under the title, "My Thousand Novel." It's clear to me now that the poems contained in that exercise were profoundly influenced by Gins's diction, by her style of description, by her digressions and elaborate meta-narrative realms, by her willingness to permit a line to go where it might. To be clear, Gins was not a writer whose books were taught at the Writers' Workshop. I doubt anyone outside of the art department would have had any idea who she was.

Something like a decade passed and I was back in New York. I was in my mid-thirties, trying to finish a PhD and working as an editor for a magazine. In an editorial meeting, a colleague mentioned Arakawa + Gins. He was interested in the Reversible Destiny project; I mentioned that I was aware of them, too. A few months later, we paid a visit to what was now the Reversible Destiny Foundation: Arakawa and Madeline had both passed away recently. We were curious about what sorts of work they might have been producing, what sorts of records existed.

This was how I came to the archive, a series of banker's boxes holding folders, typescripts, memos, printouts of websites, magazines, letters, lists, bills; materials gathered where they had been left in Gins and Arakawa's home, a building on Houston Street they had inhabited since the 1960s. There is a life's work in these cardboard containers, along with a life's accumulation of print materials and other media and ephemera. Although Gins would publish three full-length collections in her lifetime as a sole author—*WORD RAIN* in 1969, *What the President Will Say and Do!!* in 1984, and *Helen Keller or Arakawa* in 1994—she wrote a good deal more: lists, poems, essays, and experiments, including an uneven but nevertheless complete early novel (a work I have chosen not to anthologize here), along with a chapbook and multiple architectural writings co-authored with Arakawa.[13]

The list-like poetic texts I have selected from the archive seem to have existed as part of a longer work Gins titled "Transformatory Power," or "Trans-P," for short. Although this collection was never published, the work is strange and astounding. It has its affinities with some of Gins's descriptive strategies in *WORD RAIN* and *What the President Will Say and Do!!* but stands on its own as a series of examples from a period of remarkable literary experimentation Gins undertook in her 20s and 30s. I do not know why Gins never published these writings or arranged them in a final manuscript. Certainly, one might speculate that this work was ahead of its time. However, given that Gins was able to publish as complex an effort as her debut novel, it seems possible that she might have been able to find interested readers. Perhaps she simply felt that what she was attempting in these typescripts was more fully realized in the poems and sentences of *What the President Will Say and Do!!* Whatever the case may be, we now have access to these early experiments—which function like lists, through tactics of accumulation and replacement, but also seem intended to be read as poems.

In one of the most intriguing poems of the "Trans-P" series, "GHOSTING," a narrative emerges by way of discrete parts (being "ON THE SUBWAY," an

13 Gins co-authored three books with Arakawa: *Pour ne Pas Mourir / To Not to Die*, translated by François Rosso (Paris: Éditions de la Différence, 1987), *Architectural Body* (Tuscaloosa, AL: University of Alabama Press, 2002), and *Making Dying Illegal, Architecture Against Death: Original to the 21st Century* (New York: Roof Books, 2006).

"IMBROGLIO," "TEA," various actions and noises, concluding with a reflection on "LYING"). Yet this narrative, which seems to me to be at home in a sort of New Wave aesthetic, is inextricable from the work of arranging its items into a scenario, complete with actors. Note, too, that questions arise around the numbering system itself: The list begins not at "1." but at "-1.," and there are two numbers "17.," the first of which has been left blank. Item "10.," meanwhile, has been crossed out, and in item "21.," the writer appears to attempt, halfheartedly, to bracket together a set of words typed out with a good deal of space between them. The very undertaking of establishing items within the form of the list is uncertain if not fraught, and the reader has a sense of the list-maker as an important character or narrator within the disjointed story of the poem/list. Nothing could be more Ginsian: for the act of writing is folded in to the ostensible content of the written work (i.e., the narrative "action") in such a way that the two are hardly extricable. Indeed, there are parallels between the poems of "Trans-P" and the schematic, recursive poems the artist Dan Graham was making around the same time, in the late 1960s, with the significant difference that while Graham was engaged in a sort of war of attrition with respect to meaning and context, Gins's list poems invite infinite additions of meaning and context. Her writing here is schematic, yet requires that the reader not merely look at but also question the meanings of words; unlike Graham, Gins does not reduce words to their grammatical functions but rather encourages the reader to discover along with her what words will do, once they have been stripped bare of grammar. This is, after all, the affordance of a list: it provides structure and a kind of time, without resorting to the hierarchies of grammar-based sense. Lists are associative and sometimes freeing, playful. They also cannot help but evoke the deductive logic of a philosophical syllogism, an effect exploited by Gins to produce a sense of possibility and entailment in the poems of "Trans-P," something along the lines of, if "-1. ON THE SUBWAY," *then*, "1. IMBROGLIO." In other words, the plot thickens and thickens, line by line, item by item.

　　　Gins's refusal of strategies of linguistic evacuation employed by artists like Graham harkens back to the early rebus-based conceptualism of the poet Raymond Roussel (1877–1933), whose work had a profound

Schema for a set of pages whose component variants are specifically published as individual pages in various magazines and collections. In each printed instance, it is set in its final form (so it defines itself) by the editor of the publication where it is to appear, the exact data used to correspond in each specific instance to the specific fact(s) of its published appearance. The following schema is entirely arbitrary; any might have been used, and deletions, additions or modifications for space or appearance on the part of the editor are possible.

SCHEMA:

(Number of)	adjectives
(Number of)	adverbs
(Percentage of)	area not occupied by type
(Percentage of)	area occupied by type
(Number of)	columns
(Number of)	conjunctions
(Depth of)	depression of type into surface of page
(Number of)	gerunds
(Number of)	infinitives
(Number of)	letters of alphabets
(Number of)	lines
(Number of)	mathematical symbols
(Number of)	nouns
(Number of)	numbers
(Number of)	participles
(Perimeter of)	page
(Weight of)	paper sheet
(Type)	paper stock
(Thinness of)	paper
(Number of)	prepositions
(Number of)	pronouns
(Number of point)	size type
(Name of)	typeface
(Number of)	words
(Number of)	words capitalized
(Number of)	words italicized
(Number of)	words not capitalized
(Number of)	words not italicized

Above: "Schema" (March, 1966) by Dan Graham. With permission of Dan Graham.

5	adjectives
2	adverbs
69.31%	area not occupied by type
31.69%	area occupied by type
1	column
1	conjunction
no	depression of type into surface of page
0	gerunds
0	infinitives
325	letters of alphabet
25	lines
11	mathematical symbols
38	nouns
29	numbers
4	participles
8¾″ x 10⅝″	page
80 lb.	paper sheet
WEDGWOOD COATED OFFSET	paper stock
4 mil	paper
6	prepositions
10	point size type
FUTURA	type face
59	words
4	words capitalized
0	words italicized
55	words not capitalized
59	words not italicized

Above: "Schema" (March, 1966) by Dan Graham. With permission of Dan Graham.

influence on the Surrealists as well as Marcel Duchamp, particularly where Duchamp's relationship to titles was concerned.[14] As for Roussel, whose engagement with homophonic coincidences led him into lushly psychedelic fictional landscapes, Gins's reaction to the arbitrary nature of the signifier is one of fascination, followed by a determination to explore this fascinating and slightly terrifying quality of words to its very limits.[15] Gins's interest in synesthetic effects and visions related to linguistic material is, thus, something she shares with Roussel. I believe this also has something to do with what I earlier termed her "visionary cybernetics," an ardent desire to have signification carry on unfixed, via various media and means, in spite of words' (sad) tendency to delay if not halt it. I have also included two short unpublished essays from the archive as a way of showing how Gins thought about the relationship between her unique mode of experiencing images and language and her understanding of other artistic and philosophical traditions. Gins seemed to experience language in an ecstatic way, as a series of energetic sites or platforms, but at the same time was a dedicated student, reader, and researcher. Although she followed paths of her own devising, she was largely systematic, after her own fashion, and understood her art as a process of learning, with roots in empiricist approaches.

The Saddest Thing Is That I Have Had to Use Words continues chronologically, after these selections from the archive, reproducing *WORD RAIN* in its entirety and providing excerpts from the two

14 In an interview recorded in 1959 and published in *Audio Arts* magazine in 1974, Marcel Duchamp explains: "The subconscious never interested me very much as a basis for an art expression of any kind. It's true that I really was very much of a–if you could use the word–*défroqué*, or unfrocked, Cartesian, because I was very pleased by the so-called pleasure of using Cartesianism as a form of logic and very close mathematical thinking, but I was also very pleased by the idea of getting away from it. It happened also in several places in the works of Raymond Roussel, a writer who wrote these completely fantastic descriptions of the same order, where everything can be done, especially when you describe it in words, and anything can be invented–in *Locus Solus* and in *Impressions d'Afrique*. That's where, really, I found the source of my new activity in 1911 or 1912." See *Speaking of Art: Four Decades of Art in Conversation*, ed. William Furlong (London: Phaidon, 2012), 21.

15 See Raymond Roussel, *How I Wrote Certain of My books and Other Writings*, ed. Trevor Winkfield (Boston: Exact Change, 1995); John Tresch, "In a Solitary Place: Raymond Roussel's Brain and the French Cult of Unreason," *Studies in the History and Philosophy of Biological & Biomedical Sciences*, 35(2) 2004: 307-32.

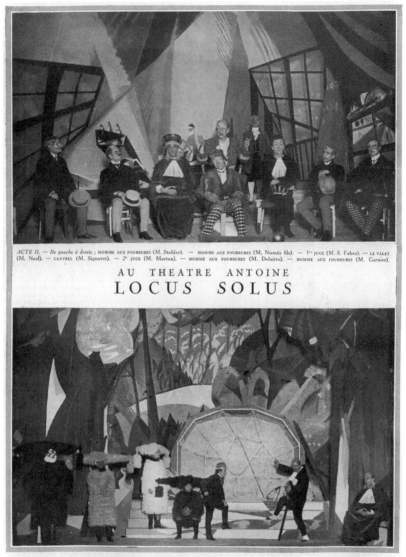

ACTE II. — De gauche à droite ; HOMME AUX FOURRURES (M. Stebler). — HOMME AUX FOURRURES (M. Numès fils). — 1er JUGE (M. S. Fabre). — LE VALET (M. Noel). — CANTREL (M. Signoret). — 2e JUGE (M. Morton). — HOMME AUX FOURRURES (M. Delaitre). — HOMME AUX FOURRURES (M. Garnier).

AU THEATRE ANTOINE

LOCUS SOLUS

ACTE Ier. — De gauche à droite ; HOMME AUX FOURRURES (M. Garnier). — HOMME AUX FOURRURES (M. Numès fils). — HOMME AUX FOURRURES (M. Stebler). — HOMME AUX FOURRURES (M. Delaitre). — NOINTEL (M. Galipaux). — CANTREL (M. Signoret). — 1er JUGE (M. S. Fabre). _Photos Gilbert-René._

Above: From an article in the January 1923 issue of *Le Théâtre et Comœdia illustré* about the Théâtre Antoine's production of Raymond Roussel's *Locus Solus* (which instigated protests and unrest).

subsequent books. Gins's writing in the selections from 1984's *What The President Will Say and Do!!* is witty, engaged, and deeply weird, whether Gins is exploring the institution of the American presidency or the concept of men, more generally. 1984's American presidential election saw Ronald Reagan and George Bush Sr.'s "Morning in America" ticket defeat Walter Mondale and Geraldine Ferraro by a whopping 525 electoral votes, with only Mondale's home state of Minnesota and the District of Columbia supporting the Democratic candidate, although Mondale won just under 41% of the popular vote.

This second-term victory for Reagan affirmed a conservative swing in the U.S.—and I think that in *What The President Will Say and Do!!* Gins becomes, in part, a writer of issue-based poetry, someone who plays with a contemporary style of meaning-making to critical ends. Although she has not altogether abandoned the formal inventions that make *WORD RAIN* so brilliant, her experiments here seem driven by a desire to influence a culture intent on sliding backward. The aphoristic injunctions and observations gathered in the long titular prose poem are absurd and sometimes impossible: "RE-ARRANGE DOGS TO WORK AS MICROPHONES." Or: "USE FIRE AS A PULLEY." Or: "INSIST ON THE TWO-DIMENSIONALITY OF THE SKY." For her hybrid essay, "All Men are Sisters," Gins employs the device of the "Dictionary of Received Ideas," a style of satirical lexicon Gustave Flaubert used to excoriating ends at the conclusion of his final novel, *Bouvard and Pécuchet*, in which familiar words receive definitions that reveal the ways in which ideology attends their use.

Thinking of this parallel, it also occurs to me to note that Gins has never been considered a "Language poet," which is to say, a participant in the American poetry and poetics movement associated with the journal *L=A=N=G=U=A=G=E*. I suppose this may have something to do with her constantly evolving way of criticizing American speech, along with her independent nature. I do not know if closer association with a literary movement would have brought Gins greater recognition for her writing during her lifetime. It remains somewhat unclear why she was never better known. Although Gins campaigned tirelessly for Reversible Destiny, her attitude to being recognized as an individual author is more difficult to ascertain.

Gins's vigorous exploration of the way words mean in a given cultural context and moment is of course closely tied to the Reversible Destiny project, which Gins and Arakawa embarked upon three years after the publication of *What The President Will Say and Do!!* in 1987. Although the project was ostensibly about intervening in the built environment to create architecture capable of combatting death, it was also an attempt to change the way in which human beings perceive and speak about the world; Gins and Arakawa argued that human acculturation leads to a dulling of the senses and, consequently, human mortality is due to a lack of sensorial stimulation and perceptual challenge. Gins's final theoretical novel of 1994 *Helen Keller or Arakawa*, excerpted at the close of this collection, illustrates some of her theories about perception related to the Reversible Destiny project. Here Gins shapes reading in a specific performative fashion, much as the allegedly "unreadable" writings of authors associated with post-structural theory such as Jacques Derrida and Jacques Lacan do. Gins's guiding metaphor for what she terms "non-visible" reading and world-apprehension here is the figure of Helen Keller, who famously learned to read and navigate the world through a process of haptic research.

A more extensive discussion of Reversible Destiny is beyond the scope of this collection and this introduction, but interested readers will find numerous resources are available. What remains lacking is a full consideration of Madeline Gins as a writer—as a poet and novelist who began, in the earliest days of popular computing in the United States, thinking through writing in a radical sense, as a process-based technology, in and of itself. It is my hope that this collection will open up a broader discussion around Gins's work, as well as the recent history of interdisciplinary practice more generally, particularly in its relation to the novel, poetry, and possible gradients between the two. I mean this in scholar Thomas Beebee's sense, i.e., that "genre is also a site of . . . noise, the cusp between different use-values of texts and between discursive entity and non-entity," as well as in Lyn Hejinian's sense of

16 Thomas Beebee, *The Ideology of Genre: A Comparative Study of Generic Instability.* (University Park, PA: Pennsylvania State UP, 1994), 17. Lyn Hejinian, "Two Stein Talks," in *The Language of Inquiry* (Berkeley: University of California Press, 2000), 105.

literary strategies that "bristl[e] with perceptibility."[16] As a high school and college student I was constantly told that novels were very important, while poetry was irrelevant to contemporary culture; that while poetry was pretty and all, it was "dead," "I, too, dislike it," and so on. Yet, what I have come to see is that the location and value of poetry was too poorly understood in these curricula: Poetry may be writing, of course, but it is not necessarily that; it is also image, performance, gesture, song, social life, gossip, furniture, food, shelter, dance, research, email, garments. This is not to say that poetry has no determined or identifiable form, but that it suffers when it is confined to a stanza. It may well need all the room of a novel, if not the room of an actual room. Madeline Gins is the one who taught me that.

Transformatory Power

Poems from the 1960s and 70s

Trans - P
'60's e 70's '

Poet : To Duchamp.

1. I am anything.
2. I will like anything
   something
4. 3 3. I anything anything.
   ~~anything~~
3. 4 4. I will chose anything
   5. Anything I choose is something.
   6.

1. _____ resting _____ went

2. _____ surface _____ went

3. _____ fallen _____ went

4. _____ space _____ went

~~Glues~~ Ode to This.

1. This is a_____

2. This is a_____

3. This is a_____

4. This is a_____

4. This_____is_____a_____

5. This_____is a_____

6. This_____is a_____ _____

7. Th_____a_____

8. This_____this_____tha_____

9. Thisis_____isis-_____isa_____

10. Thi_____s_____

A priori to you

1. A   PLACE   MAT

2. KANT'S GRATUITOUS IRRIGATION

3. PICKLED BABIES ARE BORN ALIVE

4. A TINY SKY WITH WEBBED FEET

5. THE DIRECTIONS IN A QUIET PLACE

6. A SURE GALLON

7. THE FINGER HAS A POINT

8. THE PLAN IS PLANE

9. THE (TRANSPARENT) BLOW_TORCH OF CONFUSION

10. A MAKE_DO MAKE-SHIFT

11. WEARING BANGS

12. IT IS SO WILLFUL. I MUST OBJECT

It was as if

It was as if all were/waSzzzzzzzzzzzzz,
a sheet of tranzSItivity, ISzzzzz/might be.

Theszzzzze points of (sov).

Theszzzzze telling points of.

Theszzzzze through theszzzzze.

Intension a-spring.

The next. The jack-in-the-box of

some probable point of intension.

All over the place. As the place.

Elision: on transitive of sound.

Sounds carry.

TranSItive

ziv, tziv: transitory.

YOU he sEEs it.

Seize it. Seizit. Seesit.

In the seesit.

Transeesitive.

Havi(ew)ng seen. The Sein(in)gS of it.

She does not see it. SeeSit not.

Nots,   so   many.

She SeizeS Something though.

He SeeS (seizes) it.

She sees not.

She'szzzz seizing something though.

Not may seizes it as thoroughly as he.

So that he SeeS hiS Seeing Seized.

So that he SeeS hiS Seeing Seized.

Seeing seizes her but she sees (so seizes) it not.

Is there a seeing which could seize her?

THE GEOMETRICAL PUSH

1. A STAR IN A STARE

2. THE   SEED
          BARK   OF A TRIANGLE
          VACUUM

3. THE POINT OF A MOUSE

4. THE CAUTERIZATION OF A LINE

5. A SEWING CIRCLE

6. A DEAD LINE

7. THE SHREIKS FROM A BISECTED PLANE

8. THE LONG DRAWN OUT VISIT

9. TOUCH THE RIGHT ANGLE

10. FORM FORMS FORM

SWIMMING (PLACES)

1. THE TIP OF MY TONGUE HAS_____

2. _____is inserted

3. TEN POCKETS

4. A RUBBER ARC CAUSES THE PAST TO REBOUND INDIFFERENTLY?

5. THE STRUGGLE OF LAUGHTER OR_____

6. THREADED--- ____   ____   RECEIVED ____ ____ ____

WITHOUT TITLE

1. A DRIED RAISIN LYING ON ITS BACK

2. WINGS OF SEVEN LUNGS EACH

3. FAIRY GOD   CIRCLE

4. THE FORGOTTEN SUBCUTANEOUS TRAIN
   (ALSO,WHAT IS THAT,CINNAMON,WHIPPED CREAM,
   THE CAPPUCINO)

5. THE HANDSHAKE OF FIREMEN

GHOSTING

-1.   ON THE SUBWAY

1.   IMBROGLIO

2. *Then* BURNT

3.   TEA THINGS

4.   CREW *CREW*

5.   SOON CAULKING

6.   HARD STEADY

7.   TOOK ALL THE (LOOSE) CHANGE

8.   FOUND CONCH

9.   WHIRR KICKED

10.   ~~INVOLVED IN SOMETHING~~

11. *Took a* WIPED ~~ON~~

12.   WIPED OFF WITH A DEEP VOICE

13.   MORE WHIRR

14.   MORE WHIRR

15.   AUTO OCEANOGRAPHY

16.   FELL THICK

17.

17. MATH DESK

18. FLOUR AND BURNT SECRETS

19. IN VIOL, OINTMENT'S LAWS

20. DIFFERENT SPEECHES?
    DEPTLY LYING?

21. NEW   GAUGE
    NO   GOUGE

UNMENTIONABLE OPERATION

1. SINCE CACTUS

2. SCRUB

3. BUT NEEDLES

4. TUMBLEWEED NEAR OASIS

5. A PRAIRIE

6. BUT DUNED

To Arakawa

1. Numbered hooks and eyes

2. Waterfall skin

3. A culture growth of memory

4. Oh, look you have a pencil in your hand

5. Shadow bitten

6. You are full

7. Spelling is spilling

PART

1. 111,111,111,111,111,111,111,111,111

2. 8   12   3

3. EVEN TEMPERED REACTION

4. 3 HEARTS, 5 FIRES, 7

5. SIDE EFFECTS MINUS DIGESTION

6. A SLEEPING MINUS AWAKING

7. TORTURED CLAMS PLUS RUBBER SPARKS

PLOTTING OF COURSE

1.   3

2.   2

3.   7 ALONE

4.   SPIRAL COVERS *

5.   SLASHES / THE OTHER WAY TOO

6.   A STEEL HEAD. A STEEL PENIS. NUMBERED
      DIVING BOARDS

7.   AGONIUS MINUS DEVELOPMENTIA'S FEET
      CAST IN THE SEA

* i.e. no spirals

RETRACTABLE

1. 44- 3

2. 1 $\frac{1}{1}$

3. HIS IS SEVENTY_FOUR YEARS OLD

4. 15= 1,15,000= 1, 1,500 = 1

5. ABOVE SUBTRACTION

6. 8^2+ 7-3+11+4+2-3^9+6

7. Twelved

8. THE RINSED BOTTLE NECK

9. 2 2 2 2 2

10. 6

All composing lies there

Lean your word against mine

Made in made

Only some of the importance is not trivial

A haystack of shadows looked out.

Behaving was taking place.

It preferred to remain anonymous,

but to do so it had to accept personification

just as made couldn't help itself

sounding finished.

Skill exercises while waiting for the new place.

Except connecting flushes to flourishes

sweetening the pot

juxtaposing depressions to semi-depressions

impressions march joy

and joylessness about

The remarks are still uncalled for

Start off

TO FRANCIS PONGE

1.   ALL IS ANDLESS

2.   BRICK WHEEL

3.   SHUDDER FULL

4.   CREAMER FACIE

5.   BLACK SOAP

6.   THERE IS A WORD ON YOU

How do I love Thee

Let me graph the ways

I love you past the margin of error

to where the seepage of the calculus knows to reassemble

To where parody outstrips itself

I love you diagonally as mind holds body

I love you with the chthonic union of the point

I love you with the wraith of asymptotic breath

and with the parabola which phrases speech

I love you in any transformation (as in above)

I love you as transformation

near and by

Any unit holds you

Pools,Lusions and Races

(A Curing Curve)

Less is more or less.

After all how much time is there to comb human effort?

Claire Never

next page

Suppose Lusion.

Shall we say that all points yeild allusion.

If there is a pool of allusion it is pools.

What stops function?

It won't yeild. Not this way.

If she had not worn it with a belt he would not
have married her.
The other attending day, I had "nothing to say" which
was as thick as a steak if the steak were thin.

From the to a.

Which leads to procedure.

Match the shimmerings of the pieces.

A puzzle was a pool.

The horses without the forefeet are the men.
In this pool we call them Lusions,we think of them
as a form of horse except these are without bodies.

For the pool the race is a re-thresher.

One of the fantasies is called begging the fallacy.

One of the fallacies is called begging the fantasy.

NEXT pagenext page

Two Early Essays

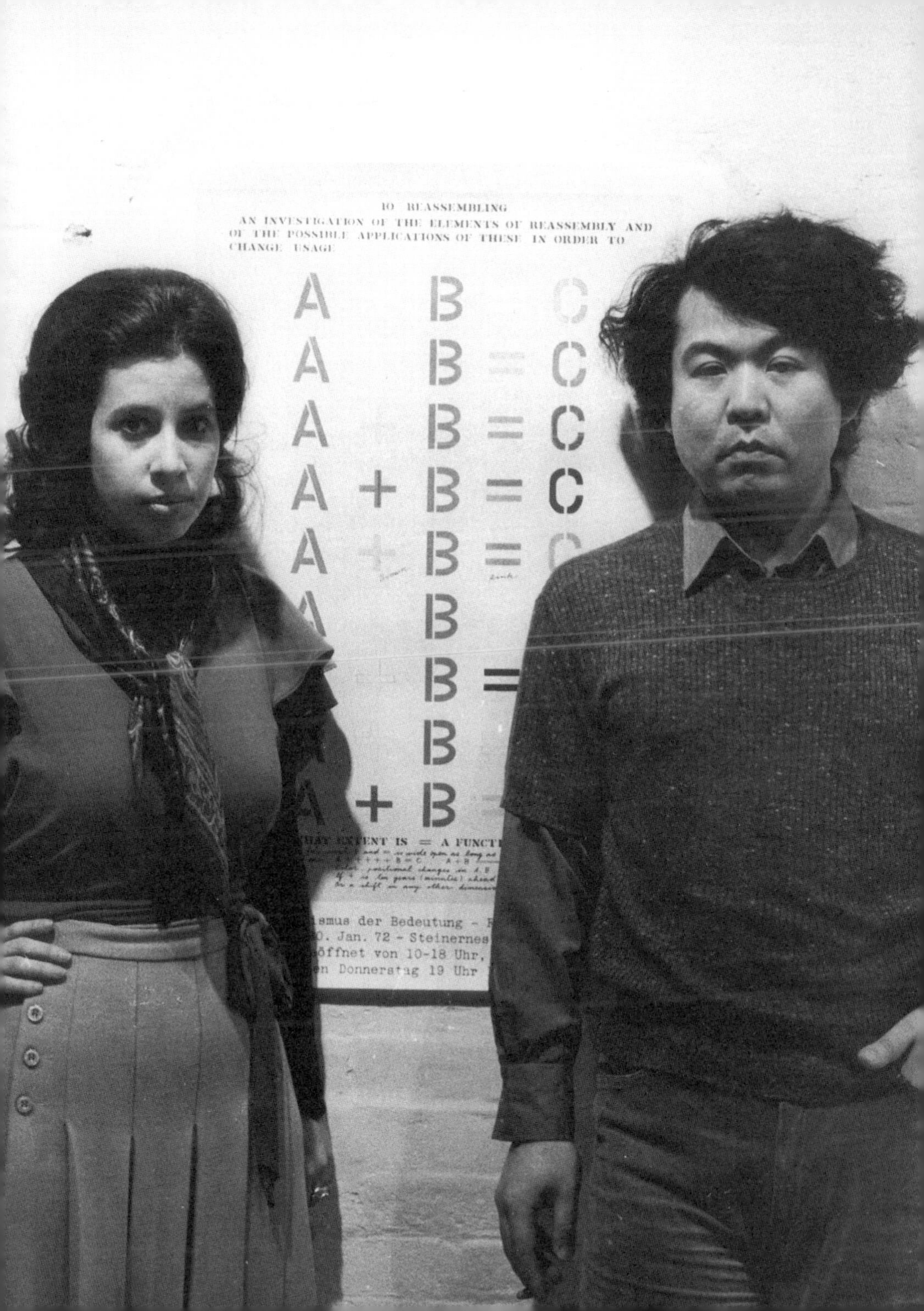
10 REASSEMBLING
AN INVESTIGATION OF THE ELEMENTS OF REASSEMBLY AND OF THE POSSIBLE APPLICATIONS OF THESE IN ORDER TO CHANGE USAGE
A B C
A B = C
A B = C
A + B = C
A + B = C
A + B
smus der Bedeutung -
0. Jan. 72 - Steinernes
öffnet von 10-18 Uhr,
en Donnerstag 19 Uhr

THE FICTIONS OF MY NON-FICTION

The images were often detailed, in color, at times revelatory, or interpretative. Sometimes they were vague, soft and cushiony. They were not always kind to me. If something faraway (across the table from me) seemed threatening, the images would let me know well. That which had siphoned off fear, also expressed it.

My eyes hardly seemed necessary. It was as if I were a road through an undulating (all containing) interior of a peach made of pictures at all different angles to each other. A sentence like "that goes there" would have its quadrant, a rub and taste (almost) of special (but unnameable) contiguity, as well as nearly mathematical implications of greater internal detail manifested as inaudible beeps that looked like short brush strokes made on air (without a brush and with only a reflection of air), all inside a yawn-shaped pocket made of Yes.

Again and again I felt the instantaneous sweep of encoding. That sweep remains as more than just memory. It feels like intuition. It may be what is called an Attitude (a predisposition?).

I became such an enraptured image viewer, that the "viewing force" (I think?) expanding, started to seem of interest to me as yet another "entity." Soon it even started to become a little critical of the images: they could say more, cover more ground. The images would have none of this. In order to dispel fear, they would have to work alone. They could not withstand a mixture of perceptual levels.

What "they" did was to step up their production. The screen was never empty. I saw a series of intriguing movies. The "viewing force," incensed, began to surface even more all the while becoming "saturated" with the fear which the images were leaving in their wake.

Although I was no longer under the rule of images, many of their terms, at least the feel of their system of approach sounded like me to me. I still felt like a receiver. I still was afraid of word intervention. I still didn't trust "outside perception." I still needed a way out of the fear. This was half the transition; the other half was Buddhism.

This is a critical essay on mental growth in the non-fictional form of autobiography. How are *fictional* transitions from one *fictional* system to another arrived at? Is it that operation, that *fictional* moment of *fictional* traction, which is actually (not nominally like this form used to express it) non-fiction? If so, how can it be made to come out in the open? But it may not be what it is.

When I was sixteen, I had read an essay about the Japanese tea ceremony which told of the concept of *shibui* (meaningful, graceful composition). It sounded like just what my images, the then ruling "force," needed. The next year I began to major in Oriental Culture. As soon as the images were gone (they've never completely gone, nor do I want them to), I seemed to understand Buddhism.

Transitions should remain always reversible. One fiction supports another, clarifies the mechanism? What we call our attitude, our angel of approach, is a mixture (a compound?) whether it is realized or not. Is the composite fictional? Of what? Only in words?

When studying Buddhism, I practiced the movableness of "I" (the giant of fiction often hidden away, cleverly concealed in non-fictional works). Once I understood that the images had been *maya* (illusions), I was informed that the "viewing force" was also a deception, although one slightly closer to the center, to *atma*, to the Buddha. Was it part of the "viewing force" which, in the encoding fashion of the images, I felt sweep into an intuition? I was given to feel (understand?) that the intuition would be able to subsume fear.

A Zen master with a huge red mustache looks at a drawing of a bodhisattva: "Why doesn't he have a red mustache?" No matter how many times I think of this koan, it is always astounding, fresh. If the image *is* the master's vision, why isn't it complete? With one question he indicates that he is very careful of details but not careful of them. He points out the humor, in the face of all we don't know about ourselves, of individuality. Is he thinking of the arbitrary nature of the rest stops provided by matter and energy for perception? Is it that perception just does not perceive enough?

Or is this just an idle question thrown out at random from the sheer joy of beatitude? Is it a way to point out the meaninglessness of certain philosophical questions? (Moore and Wittgenstein in one sentence?) No particular weight is given to any *one* position.

I will try to demonstrate in the fiction of non-fiction that systems incorporate as they replace one another; to speak according to only *one* is a fallacy, or at least an incomplete statement. If whatever becomes Attitude is a compound (mixture?), it may require many systems, cross-fictional semantic readings, to bring it out in the open.

I thought of that koan again when I saw Delvaux's nudes with big, pink ribbons on their breasts and when I saw Magritte's painting of a torso which was a face. There is also the slight image or feeling of a red mustache (just the inner edge of it) when I put into effect the meaning of the term "hypostatize."

I decided to become a painter. I just didn't want to put aside the images. The koans had taught me to see then see through. Did I want to see if I could before I did?

I met Arakawa.

From his suggestions and kindness I began to repossess the images (re-order the fear?) to make them suit cognitive as well as affective needs. How in the world did I do that? Another transition occurred; it happened.

I painted a series of babies with carrots coming out of their heads. If this could happen, it would change everything, so I called these "The New Baby Jesus." By painting an off-balance child, I steadied my own balance. (?) A child with a carrot of "home-grown" variety in its head would simply have another kind of balance (internal and external) from what humans knew so far. I found it exciting to think that this would require an essential alternation of the genes. Then with the Root evident right there on top of his head, what else would become more apparent? Was it that a new basis would make things easier to understand? But this was a guess not really a new basis. As long as I favored it, it offered relief, but as a wild guess which required a single-minded belief, it was only a temporary measure, one which could never offer a systematic attack on the roots of fear.

To believe in any *one* system alone is a giant fiction, one which leads to dogmatism. Such a believer, despite whatever subtlety of his thought (his fiction), is an uncritical man. Hans Vaihinger thought of Kant's *Ding an Sich* as the greatest of fictions. It is in the movement from one fiction to another, from one system of fiction to another, that the critical view is possible. That is the context in which hypothesis can occur. And it is within changing contexts such as that, that analysis and description are possible.

I had learned to shift some of the weight to find relief from "a part of the fearful pressure." The externalized images as a symbol was quite absorbent for some time. Practice such as this made it possible for me to begin to look at Arakawa's paintings with understanding and for another transition to occur.

Arakawa's Painting, *Diagram of Part of the Imagination*: A Non-Fictional Working Out of Fictions (1963–64)

Diagram of Part of the Imagination (6'x4') is a floor plan drawn with supplementary lines to indicate movement. Each room has its name stenciled in. Some of the names were also drawn (not written) to indicate movement. Color is used to give schematic reality to qualitative changes from place to place.

There are two other Arakawa paintings which somehow contributed to the "supporting" context which permitted me to enter this one. *S.A. Equation* is a diagram of the hypothetical case of a ship's passage through land. *Bottomless* is a diagram of a hollow rectangular "cone" with its tip missing; within this, a grid is drawn. As the grid is drawn down through the shape, it continues to further subdivide toward infinity through and/or into what is bottomless (Are these *Separated Continuums*? This is the title of another Arakawa painting of that period.).

Bottomless is a series. In one version of it, a dot appeared toward the bottom of the grid, an arrow led to what could be thought of as one of its names: grandmother. In view of this addition, which way now could the dividing grid be thought to be progressing? Down toward the past or toward the future? Progressions are usually assumed to move toward the future. But "grandmother" has the ring of the past to it. Was the grid dividing toward the past so reuniting toward the future? Or was it a question of neither of these? In any case, where was that dot supposed to be located? The specifying of one aspect of the dot's original context had the surprising effect of causing the overall context, that of the subdividing grid, to become all the more movable, open to speculation.

Was it that memory was being evoked within the depiction of its dissolution? Or was the dot merely evidence of the stain which any living might leave on a continuum through which it had existed? Or by putting into the sign system of line, color, shape, just one element of that other written language, by so precisely locating "grandmother" within the logic of the subdividing grid, was Arakawa hoping to have the mechanism(s) of our written and spoken language come to be evoked, remembered, and perceived in terms of what was diagrammed? In other words, could not the creation of any language be thought of as a subdividing process, synchronic as well as diachronic?

Arakawa destroyed that painting. Either I never asked him why or I don't remember what he told me when I did. Such a lapse in communication is unusual in our relationship. Perhaps it is better left where it is to "germinate" within the context of memory. It has a "force" all its own. Does Memory assume a special cast at the moment (place?) it assumes (feels?) what it has forgotten? What part does fiction play in forgetting? A dynamic one? Inverted?

It is posited by the title, *Diagram of Part of the Imagination*, that which comprises the act of perceiving the painting (such mechanism and effects) is not only present in what is seen but is diagrammed there as well. If the diagram is there at all, it operates as a diagram of that part of the imagination which envisions it. It is the source and subsequent evidence of the imagination's act of "hypostatizing" itself around perceptual information to give it a sense of "reality."

Arakawa intends to *point out* not *say*; he is able to do this by using a combination of sign systems. He gives an hypothesis to which the act of imagining, thinking, may coincide. He may be thought of as a realist or more accurately, an analytic pragmatist.

This painting of a floor plan may be used as a key (skeleton key?) to the viewing situation. Suppose the viewing takes place in the bedroom:

Begin by looking at the bedroom part of the diagram. This locates the viewer in the bedroom in several ways. In terms of the "realism" of which I've just spoken, the viewer becomes aware of that part of the imagination by which he has been (and is) sketching out (feeling out) the "actual" room; he may begin to restructure or map this feeling in relation to the painted bedroom which a part of the imagination may (usually does?) superimpose on the original. The newly imagined painted bedroom may serve as a grid (movable) against which to measure the sites of the original, "actual" one.

Next when the viewer reads the stenciled-in word BEDROOM into the actualizing situation, it tends in such a situation to emphasize the separations of referend (Attitude? Feeling? Part of the Imagination?) from referent (written word) and reference ("actual" room). This might serve to make more apparent the process which allows for these elements to function as a unit.

When the diagram is seen as a whole from the vantage point of the bedroom, the viewer then actualizes the rest of the apartment within the perspective of his memory. In this way the movable grid, now probably superimposed on a collection of memories, may serve as a precursor of the realism which will ensue once the viewer begins to move into the other rooms. Then, as he moves, the mechanism of that diagramed part of the imagination is reenacted each time from a different angle, a new context. In what way do these contexts come to be mixed?

Arakawa paints his compounds of sign systems to human scale. This has a strange, significant effect: on one hand, it increases the debt to fiction (invention or imaging of an event, statement, or occurrence); on the other, it provides a new context in which signs of the written language, enlarged, begin to point out the fictionalizing nature of their own system. Words become so familiar that the reader sometimes forgets what it was that they were to be counted on for. Seen in a new context, an enlarged one, a word may lose some of its "dogmatic" presence and work more as an "irritating presence"; it may thus be employed to expound to some extent on its own nature.

Some of what I've said will describe the viewing of *any* painting, but all the differences come from the fact that Arakawa is one of the few painters who talks (paints) in terms of hypothesis, a composite of sign systems (fictions) rather than choosing *one* fiction from among many.

WORD RAIN
(or A Discursive Introduction to the Intimate Philosophical Investigations of G,R,E,T,A, G,A,R,B,O, It Says)

complete facsimile reproduction of the original

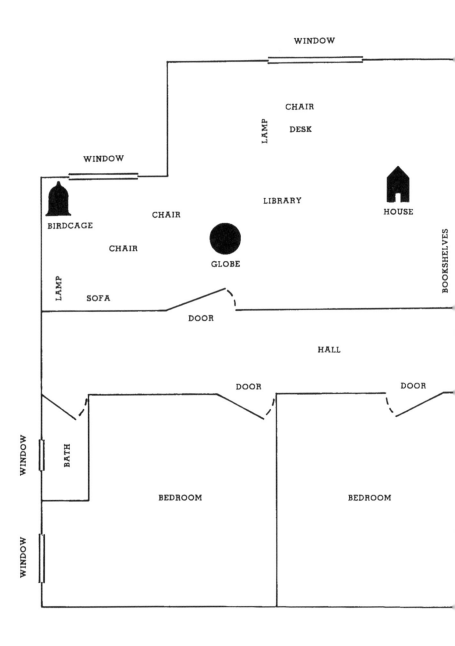

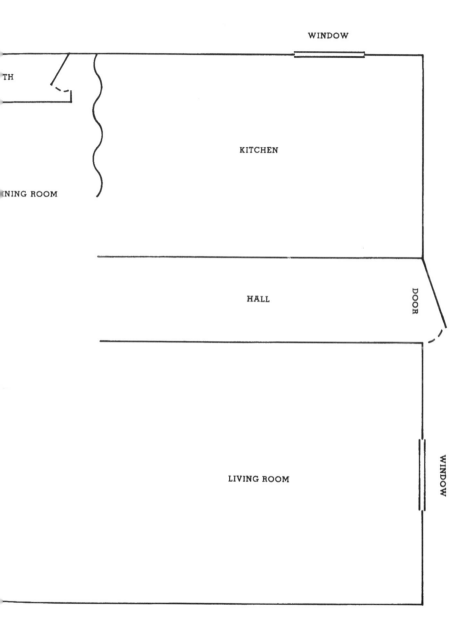

WINDOW

TH

KITCHEN

NING ROOM

HALL

DOOR

LIVING ROOM

WINDOW

WORD RAIN

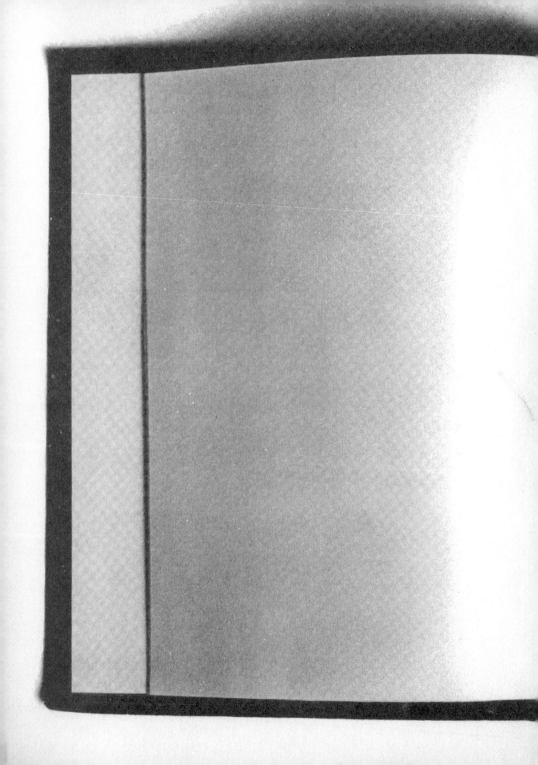

WORD RAIN

OR

A DISCURSIVE INTRODUCTION

TO

THE INTIMATE PHILOSOPHICAL INVESTIGATIONS

OF

G,R,E,T,A, G,A,R,B,O,

IT SAYS

MADELINE GINS

GROSSMAN PUBLISHERS   NEW YORK   1969

To ~~the universe for the existence of~~ Arakawa   E. M.

Typography and design by Samuel N. Antupit.

The author expresses her gratitude to the following for permission to include copyright material: to J. M. Dent & Sons, Ltd. and the Trustees for the Joseph Conrad Estate for the quotation from LORD JIM by Joseph Conrad; to Grosset & Dunlap, Inc. for the quotation from LITTLE WOMEN by Luisa May Alcott; to Grove Press, Inc. for quotations from THE ERASERS by Alain Robbe-Grillet and from STORIES & TEXT FOR NOTHING by Samuel Beckett; to Hamish Hamilton, Ltd. for the quotation from ACCOUNT UNSETTLED by Georges Simenon; to Harcourt, Brace & World, Inc. for the quotation from MRS. DALLOWAY by Virginia Woolf; to Houghton Mifflin Co. and Allen & Unwin, Ltd. for the quotation from THE TALE OF GENJI by Lady Murasaki; to Macmillian & Co. for the quotation from CRIME AND PUNISHMENT by Fyodor Dostoevsky; to New American Library, Inc. for quotations from THE RETURN OF THE NATIVE by Thomas Hardy and MOBY DICK by Herman Melville; to The Philosophical Library for quotations from BEING & NOTHINGNESS and A CRITIQUE OF PURE REASON by Jean-Paul Sartre; to The Ronald Press Co. for the quotation from GULLIVER'S TRAVELS by Jonathan Swift; to The Something Else Press, Inc. for the quotation from THE MAKING OF AMERICANS by Gertrude Stein; to Time/Life Books for the quotation from BEND SINISTER by Vladimir Nabokov; to The Viking Press, Inc. for the quotation from "The Dead" from THE DUBLINERS by James Joyce originally published by B. W. Huebsch, Inc., in 1916, copyright © 1967 by the Estate of James Joyce; to A. Watkins, Inc. for a quotation from THE AGE OF INNOCENCE by Edith Wharton, © 1920 by D. Appleton Co., renewal © 1948 Wilbain R. Tyler.

All the care possible has been taken to obtain permission from the copyright owners to reprint the quotations protected by copyright; any errors or omissions are unintentional and will be rectified in any future printings upon notification to the author.

1.

The Waterfall
or
An Introduction

I induce a sly birth with my eyes the lines of creases. (Delete) I massage geometry with a scented oil. The maintenance of lips. The battles of containers. I speak in the midst of a sifted reticence. Over there in the center, I am imploded as the size of a fly. Words fall off the curls of nothing after I have left for the next moment.

I am folded into her. I am involved in the curves of her grey folds. I know how to use them. I know better now than at first but I knew then too. She moves as I shift. Words rain on a molded juncture which you might mistakenly call my head.

I fill her up at the typewriter. I move her femininely as befits her body. I take her with me. I introduce the tensile subject into her. I am her introduction to the room, to the word rain, to the waterfall pummeling down over membranous rocks. I find her room. I move in the damp ocean. Words cannot say how I am she.

I am not afraid to move. I am the judge. It is raining in the ocean. I am a river of hypotheses, categories and disjunctive relations. I pulled Aristotle taught. I wave them and words tumble out. They eddy into sentences with my meaning. Read this with me, read that with me, read me with me, read objects (tables,toes,toads, tails,tin,trains,type,tears,throat) read write read right. This is still life. Only I write and read. If you've misplaced me on your own, bring me up again from off this page.

I must say that (even though it is entirely possible that I originate a million miles from here) I am closer than this book which is very close. I give you this book for a present. It comes with a room, light, a country, sky and weather. I will arrange for you to be made aware of these in detail. You may look at everything. You will see only what I see. Look at this sentence. There is nothing on it. Now look at this sentence. I see a plate of desert ribbed with dunes held in place with drops of slime just above a layer of petrified tentacles. There is nothing in this sentence. I say I see a book in this sentence. Without me, it words the page; yet says nothing.

Words. I have my secrets even to myself at times. Ludwig W. tried to remove the "if." I am a word. Any word pick any word. Which leads us to my secret. Even I have to stop and think how to say something at times. I might finally be wordless. I will not say. I am the liar the one who says I am not telling the truth.

I have shown her who soon through my pretense will pretend to be me, how to freshen up words by bringing them into my presence. She will apply these to my circumstances: waft,platform,quay,rostrum,ropy gas shavings,fibers. Later on (Chapter 6) lists of words will appear and demand an application. Any word may apply. Other words are: read,mist,now,book,came,continue, remember,finish. Notice how these find their range and limits only within my presence.

The more possibilities are suggested, the more possibilities exist, the more possibilities are taken in by the imagination, the more the imagination's possibilities are defined, the more the possibility of more possibilities can be recognized. The possibilities of more possibilities lead to the imagination itself, immediately and to me. Only after this will you be in the position to start making charts to help you know how you know where you are when you get somewhere.

I walk through my perceptions, keeping the distance. I am the only one who can decide to breathe. I will help her and you when you practice to be me. When you see [f] I say breathe fast; [s] slow breathing; [m] through the mouth;

ⁿ you will breathe through your nose; ᵛᶠ very fast, you are right; ᵛˢ very slow, you are right; ʰ hold your breath. Each notation governs 1/8 of a minute unless otherwise noted. If you had known this at the beginning of this paragraph this paragraph would have been made to contain 7/8 of a minute of breathing in 1/8 of a minute of reading. If there is no notation on the page, breathe any way you like, just be sure not to die. No matter how many mistakes you make I will hold our breath. I am that which knows what to do.

Even now this is a sound book. It moves through my hum. I take the letter b and move it toward ack, it moves back into me. h has become involved with as. Needless to say t, l, r, d, s, w, b, c, and v may become involved with ent, etc. Every letter that I see has been sounded at least two times. So too every word has been lived, although I must sadly admit that I do not know any living word besides myself which is a secret.

One joke is that I must do everything at least twice in order to communicate. I must think and say and then hear and think. I lisp around my secret, my thinking is sinking. In order to isolate myself as the process of thinking, I must think of thinking or more conveniently read my reading. This is an extensive joke in the manner of the irony of names, the belly laugh of birth or the Chaplinesque persistence of consciousness.

Let me clear your throat. I symbolize your existence for you as I read your life. I have taught her that the poet should be the first to extend herself. And for the dumber (those who have had less practice in talking to themselves) it is now being said that living is almost reading.

Words. Here is a selection of words. The selection of words has been made but is no longer here. There is the selection of the words themselves. I must face them. They face each other. It will be seen that the word TOUCH is facing itself (and it may be imagined to do what it says when the book is closed). She has faced them and positioned them in relation to me. Face them, but if at the point of unheard-of intimacy detachment is felt to be required I will fold the imagination over the process of reading itself .... fold along the dotted line and tear, making sure, of course, that the cutting-off points fall within the last quarter (3/4 of the way in) of the internalization process. I am thinking of you. I must always think of you and scribble in your outline. I write you. I read you. And it seems furthermore that I must read and write for you.

I wrote her and read her to her before she wrote this book. Except for a few insertions I left her on her own (TOUCH) except to be with her every instant. I have made investigations into her language. I have investigated the means of her disposal. I have preserved these in oiled geometry, liniment algebra and creamed mathematics in hope that they will not become mixed with the word rain.

In the paragraph above, let

A = the first sentence B = the second C = the third
D = the fourth E = the fifth

P indicates paragraph W = word $, = ,$ (identity)
M = meaning M' = further meaning

$A = 13W + M_1$ $B = 18W + M_2$ $C = 7W + M_3$
$D = 8W + M_4$ $E = 24W + , + M_5$

$P = 70W + , + (M_1 \ldots M_5)$ would be an incorrect statement

Rather $P = 70W + , + (M_1 \ldots M_5) + O + M'$

(by self-evidence $, = $ pause$— , = 1W$)

$P = 71W + (M_1 \ldots M_5) + O + M$

W = word   O = zero   E = mc²   M = meaning

$$W + E + O = M$$
$$\underline{-M} \qquad \underline{-M}$$
$$W + E + O - M = O \text{------} *W + E + O - M = O$$
$$\underline{-O} \qquad \underline{-O}$$
$$W + E - M = O$$

$$W - M = O - E \text{-------} *W - M = O - E$$
$$W = O - E + M \text{-------} *W = O - E + M$$

By substitution:

$$P = 71 \, (O—mc²=M) + [(W+mc²+O)_1 \dots (W+mc²+O)_5)]$$
+ M′ + O would most closely represent the situation

Org (x) means   x is an organic unit

Yxy   means   Organic unit x is transformed into organic unit y (i.e. x divides into several parts of which one is y [cell division] or fuses with one or more units to produce y [cell fusion])

Orgs. (x)   x is an organism

⊃ means   if something then something

⊂ means   subclass or subrelation

Axioms
1. Org (x) ⊃ Th (x)   Each organic unit is a thing
    Org ⊂ Th

2. The members of Y are organic units:
    Yxy ⊃ Org (x)   Org (y)
    Mem (y) ⊂ Org

I taught her just as I had taught Marcel D. to cross out a few large sections that are relatively unimportant (important for D.) yet pertinent to the text to establish in still another way a) interest b) levels of consciousness c) perspective d) degrees of intimacy of the writer with the writing e) confusion and guilt, the subcurrents of the imagination in the reader.

Confusion is a word. Words are our confusion. Read and be confused. But don't be just a little confused. A great confusion follows just as she who let me speak will now speak as me but through her with a different I which will still for the most part be me. To paraphrase Nietzsche (as well I might) the greatest confusion lives in the house. A meeting of confusions. Yet I am the only one who will read this book.

I hope that I can say that I will never say good-bye to you. I did. With great hope for your eternal presence in the future . . .

The saddest thing is that I have had to use words.

— — — — — — read — — — — — — — — —
— — — — — — — — — — — — — — — — —
— — — — — — — — — — — — — — — — read
— — — — — — — — — — — — — — — — —
— — — — — — — — — — — — — — — — —
— — — — — — — — — — — — — — — — —
— — — — — — — — — — — — — — — — —
— — — —
— — — — — — — — — — — — — — — — —
— — — — — — — — — — — — — — — — —
— — — — — — — — — — — — — — — — —
— — — — — — — — — — — — — — — — —
— — — — — — — — — — — — — — — — —
— — — — — —
— — — — — — — — — — — — — — — — —
— — — — — — — — — — — — — — — — —
— — — — — — — — — — — — — — — — —
— — — — — — — — — — — — — — — — —
— — — — — — — — — — — — — — — — —
— — — — — — — — — — — — — — — — —
— — — — — — — — — — — — — — — — —
— — — — — — — — — — — — — — — — —
— — — — — — — — — — — — — — — — —
— — — — — — — — — — — — — — — — —
— — — — — — — — — — — — — — — — —
— — — — — — — — — — — — — — — — —
— — — — — — — —
— — — — — — — — — — — — — — — — —
— — — — — — — — — — — — — — — — —
— — — — — — — — — — — — — — — — —
— — — — — — — — — — — — — — — — —
— — — — — — — — — — — — — — — — read.

2.

The Introduction
of the Waft
or
Paraphrased
Sensibility

I reached for a cookie just as I reached for the third page in search of an extremely long sentence which was pouring over onto it from the second one. In it, it was told how everything was retrieved after a short scuffle which turned out to be about nothing at all.

A worm twisted up into the weather. Let's pause for a moment.

On this page the author wanted to make it known that his two preceding pages were perfect examples of how he did not intend to write the rest of the book. He said that it was entirely possible, almost certain, that two microphytic colonies of bacteria had settled on the blank pages, twisted their tiny bodies into male and female letters and had remained there, clinging to those pages for dear life, even before he had had a chance to get started. He spoke of having allowed them to remain only as evidene. The author then cautioned his reader to smell each page as a simple yet sufficient precaution against being taken in in the future. He assured this same reader that although the odor of these microphytic letter heads and bodies was indescribable, it was nonetheless distinct and unforgettable. He said that touching the page would be no help at all but that the smell would always and immediately give them away.

The page slipped through my fingers. It slipped into the bottom drawer of the desk, which was only slightly open. It wasn't the letter signed Mary Tassler nor the ~~notice from Life magazine that it was time for renewal.~~ ~~I put those back and reached into the drawer again.~~ ~~My fingers touched something moist and rubbery. It~~ ~~wasn't difficult to pick that up. It was a gum eraser. I~~ ~~transferred it to my left hand and put my right hand in~~ ~~again to pull out the third page. As I was finishing that~~

page I pulled the gum eraser along the polished edge
of the desk. I heard a hum from across the room and
remembered that there was a bird in a cage near the
other window.

Up until entrance into the room with the box, I was
shifting about in my chair to get into a more comfortable
position.

Little drops of moisture slipped around and down
my neck in that hot early summer afternoon as ahead
of me I allowed the print to filter through the sticky
room into view.

The light kept hitting
page in front of me
people were trying
being interested in
gift which still sat
table with a reddish brown
having passed through and
paper) fluid dripping from
bottom corner on the right
(the side closest to the
having had the impression
in it which had just
as she had taken it from
felt it to be some sort
which was breaking but also
its shape because of its

I
knew
that
the
other
man
would
return
in
about
ten
minutes
to
offer
me
lunch

and resting on the
in which four tired
not to make a point of
opening the unasked-for
on the rickety hall
grainy (perhaps for
mixed with the brown
the worn-through
side of their view
door). Mary spoke of
there was something
cracked. She said that
the messenger she had
of glass container
more or less keeping
tight wrappers.

I skimmed over the conversation as it flowed on over the page.

"Of — — — — — — to — — — — that — — — made for sure — — — — — — — — ask — — — — — —."

"I — — — — yet — — — — — — with you — — — —."

"— — — — not — — — — reason — — — — — — —."

"— — — — — still — — — meant — — — — — — — because — — — — not — — — — — — time — — — across — — — — think so?"

"— — — — — — — — — — — — — to me!"

"— — — — — — — — — — — you?"

"— — — — — — — calm — — — — —."

"— — — — — — tomorrow — — — — — — — better — — — — — — — — so?"

"— — — — — — — — expect — — — — the — — — with — — — — — — — — — — — — — — not?"

"— — — — — — — — — hero."

"— guess — — — — choice in the — — — — — —."

"— — — — — — — — about — — — gain — — — — — — eat."

"— — — — idea!"

The man was coming down the hallway. My hand left my mouth, opened the top button of my blouse, went as far as it could inside it, scratched and came out as the man came in. I looked up and buttoned up my blouse.

"Are you ready for lunch? How's it going?"

"I'm only on the fifth page. It's interesting."

"What should I tell Judy?"

"O.K."

The man walked around the desk to stand just behind me. His shadow fell onto the page. Now the sun poured down only onto the floor.

In the cool shadow which the man's head cast on the page, I read [vf] the pale grey letters as they turned into and about the need for an accompanying letter. The people there couldn't understand why it had not arrived with the package. It would come tomorrow.

I sensed that as I read the word "letter," the phrase "not yet received [vs] the letter" — the man [vf] read "purpose," "it could not have been on purpose." When I finally caught "purpose" the man had "fingers" — "Mary's pale fingers" on his mind. I hopped off "purpose" heading immediately for "fingers" which I'd already peeked at and taken up inside me. The sixth page had the sense to it of a letter which had been delayed.

As the man walked away the clear vision of the sun searchlighted the page. Halfway across the room, the man turned to face me. ~~He stood there skewered on his own beam of light as was I in mine. His lips stretched to open and seemed to mouth several words before he spoke. He trembled a step backwards. He stood on his two legs. He thoughtlessly balanced himself in that library of that third-floor apartment. The weight of the moment tipped the scale. He careened into an expression on his face.~~ It was possible that thousands of microphytic bacteria made up his outline. The smell was unforgettable. What I saw had been written before even as it was being written now. For my own part, I think it came to him suddenly. His density, in every sense — that is, in the photographic [vs]: an opaque quality or the amount of light-stopping material; in the electrical: the amount of electricity flowing through a unit of area in a unit of time; and in the physical: the ratio of the mass of an object to its volume — his density rose up as a whole unit expressed in a real number and rose up straight out of his shoes.

"Interesting piece, isn't it?"

The sun was poured on him. It settled into both of us. It crept right through the library window, through intangible crevices, down onto our molded membranes and was absorbed through the acrobatic mush of our living to sink into each of us as a variety of infra-red supportive hands which hugged and pushed in among other places beneath the diaphragm; and thus, similarly, across this room in two separate cases, the sun once again defined a somehow familiar comfort (of sorts).

"I suppose so."

The man squinted and brought his hand up to shield his eyes.

"I hope the little birthday party that Judy's preparing for Linda in the ⁵ dining room isn't going to disturb you. We just couldn't call it off. I'll try to keep the lid on it."

"If you could just come in when she b̶ ̶ ̶ ̶out the candles . . . Lunch is almost ready. I'll br̶ ̶ ̶ ̶re."

Step by step, maintaining a good balan̶ ̶ ̶ ̶t along, the man left the room to me.

Page seven felt a little heavier than the oth̶ on it: " 'Don't touch it. It wouldn't be fair,' Ma̶ worth admonished," was the first sentence there̶ were on their way into the dining room where a ̶ snack was waiting. They had agreed not to open th̶ package until the letter had arrived. A man who had been taking a rest upstairs called down that he'd be there in a moment, but he didn't come down until the bottom of the page.

I changed pages and picked the outer reaches of my nose. . . .

The sun poured in through the window behind me. It hugged my shoulders as I leaned back into it and read some more.

~~The author wanted to make it clear that it had actually all started on an afternoon in June~~. The doorbell had rung. No one there had felt he should answer it. Each in turn felt it wasn't his place. The ringer was persistent. Finally, Mary Lampworth headed for the door. It was, as they'd suspected, not a guest, only a delivery. They put the medium-sized box on the hall table. It remained there untouched for the rest of the day. They thought that it might have been sent by someone who had just had breakfast. There were bits of dried egg along the folds of the brown paper wrapping.

The sun shone brightly and particularly on the two words "hall table." I sensed the man tiptoeing out of the room. My hand floated up to my tongue again. Swiftly I began to lick it as I nearly thoughtlessly settled back into the page of letters <u>wafting</u> through my eyes.

As I translated the characters into the myste_____ of clarity, of logical sequence, I interpreted m___ weighted position, sealed in a chair, overshad____ these noted lives, my own position in the light of th___ in view of the circumstances, in line with my reas___ I was, roughly, a folded five foot three inch (in ___ directions: five inch, one foot) tissue covering eigh___ ten operating systems all of which appeared to funct___ finally to give me an edge on the waft.

"I suppose so," I said. I noticed that my hand ha___ crumpled the page of the manuscript and smudged___ several words off into oblivion.

The little droplets of letters gathered into word puddles on the pages. I is slipping out of me.

~~In the morning and up until the late part of the early afternoon, it was a clear and sunny day. A man got out of his car not forgetting a generous tip for the doorman. Even so, at that moment the sun slipped into a cloud pocket. "Now darlings," she said in the year B.C., "there is still time for lunch." There was a gift sitting on the a priori table of contents in the ontologically spontaneous passageway. Oscar Wilde had a well known figure in moving pictures. A bunch of neighborhood kids who hang like grapes off the braided tonguelike vine of infinite sadness are being tough with each other. Judy is making an invisible lunch. Linda is becoming seven years old. My breath is leaving me.~~ Microphytic bacteria live long deaths. They just said that and one of them is urging a group of them on to say: "I am the living word."

All the walking that has been done has been along the hypotenuse. The four enormous inclined planes contain innumerable subdivisions. Liquids were told to flow down these. Anything else we perceive is only apparent.

~~Not every projector has enough light or film. Once one child got only one slide. It is sometimes advantageous to work through a microphytic agent.~~

A root touched bottom. Let's pause for a moment.

I put the gum eraser in the bird's cage so it could clean its behind while it ' sharpened its beak on the cuttlestone.

The sun shone dully on that eraser, on the front side of the desk which was facing into it, on the pile of papers, on most of the words of the page which I had in my hand, in the corners of the room and on all the books in the shelves except those nearest the door. It shone particularly brightly on the word guess and distinctly though a little less so on the words: try, then, after, window, pass me, can't, not so, hall and inside which were [s] all on the eighth page; it also dwelled brightly on the middle of my ring, my finger, just below the rim of the cup, the five or six corner bars of the bird's cage, the handles of the desk [vs] drawers, on the crown of my head, off the plumpest part of a big leather chair on the other side of the L-shaped library and on the farthest right-side corner from the sun's point of view or what would be the nearest corner on the left from the vantage point of the door. On this last part, the sun seemed to just spread out like butter on a warm piece of light toast. (That tasty morsel would soon be slipped into the mouth of a storm.)

"Don't leave me behind . . ."

As I read on, the phrase, "on the corner of Sepulveda and . . ." wafted into mind. "And now the shouts waft near the citadel" Dryden. The enormous weight of the waft which was quite light was the thing that kept me contained in my perfect state which was as good as the state of any other thing before it is broken.

"Absolutely — — — — — —!"
"— — — — — — case, — — — — — — — — — — —
— leave."
"Not — — — — — — — life — — — — —."
"— — you — — — any — — — — — — — —
— — — saying?"
"Oh — — — —, isn't — — — — — — touching!"
"Let's — — — — — — — — — least."
"— — — not?"

These words were coming down the hall:

"No, you go tell her. I'm too busy. —— she'll under-stand. Here and bring her this. The rest will be ready in a couple of minutes. I'm just waiting for the toast. Say hello for me and make my apologies."

I heard the dull paired tones of footsteps walking down the hall and felt them head toward me, toward the library. I shifted the bulk of my understanding from one side to the other as I waited for my host to become my guest.

I picked up the glass paperweight just as the man reached the doorway and indicated that he would come in.

Interesting piece, isn't it. "Yes." The man's density had shifted. This might have been because (among other things) much of the sunlight had <u>wafted</u> away. He was carrying a variety ~~of treats on the very same tray with which he had brought the tea and which he had managed to return to the kitchen and reload without my having even been aware of its absence.~~

I had kept my finger glued to the corner of page nine, when the man had thoughtlessly placed the tray on top of the pile of papers. Now I closed my fingers about that corner, pulled on the paper and succeeded in slipping it out from under.

I held the page in front of me. I handed the paper-weight to the man who was now standing behind me. The man played with the paperweight as he stood behind me and read over my shoulder.

"I just want to finish this chapter."

Again I sensed that as my pair of eyes hit on "window" — the phrase — "near ^{vf} the window" — the others were up to "table" — "resting on the table." When I finally slipped and slid down to "table" the others were already on "made" — "the only deduction to be made" or on "as far as they could see." As I skipped ahead to "see" the others took in "guess" — "it was the first guess," and went right on to "ready" — "everybody was ready." As I looked up from the last page of the first chapter, I felt that everybody was now ready for a guessing game. I put the paper down and took up a spoon. The man held onto the back of my chair as I cut off a big spoonful of melon. The sun bit the dust ^{n} in back of me.

Read
Punctual organs
Glass   Paper   Weight
As a matter of fact
It is fitting
A root touched its bottom
As the waft shifts
it turns out to be breath
Interesting piece, isn't it?
A microphytic colony
drank a cup of tea
in less than one second
it became it.
The last word
The last word is a brace
          Read

$$P = \text{page} \quad W = \text{word} \quad A = \text{attention}$$
$$G = \text{a group of words}$$
$$P = 300W$$
$$P + A = A\,(G) + 300\,W - G$$

In order for P to be read we must have the situation of P — P brought about by A. This would enable us to consider the operation complete and to turn the page.

$$G = 3\,W$$
$$P + A = A\,(3\,W) + 300\,W - 3\,W$$
$$P + A = 3\,W\,A + 297\,W$$

$$A = 3\,W\,A + 297\,W - P$$

$$(P = 300\,W)$$

$$A = 3\,W\,A + 297\,W - 300\,W$$
$$A = A\,W\,A - 3\,W$$

The operation can continue IFF (if and only if)
$$A = A^2 = A^3$$

$$(A^2)\ A = 3\,W\,A - 3\,W\,(A^2)$$
$$A^3 = 3\,W\,A^3 - 3\,W\,A^2$$
$$\text{iff } A^3 = A^2$$

then:
$$A^3 = A^3\,(3\,W - 3\,W)$$
$$100\,A^3 = 100\,A^3\,(3\,W - 3\,W)$$
$$*100\,A^3 = A^3\,(300\,W - 300\,W) \text{ or } (P - P)$$

The page has been read.

reAd

3.

A.

Reading in the Rain
or
The Multiplication
of Consciousness

B.

More
or Later

I thought, No, later.

The chewed up chunks of melon fell through the
The chewed up chunks of melon fell through the
gorge vs past the rostrum, down the deep narrow pass
through the steep heights. The speaker at the rostrum
through the steep heights. The speaker at the rostrum
asked to be left alone. I walked on out past the reader's
asked to be left alone. I walked on out past the reader's
quay, through the right-angled L-shaped room, along
quay, through the right-angled L-shaped room, along
the wooden plane nailed into position according to the
the wooden plane nailed into position according to the
axes of the room. The waft ebbed and flowed against
the quay.

As I pushed the first page of the second chapter be-
tween my sticky fingers, I remembered that I had read
the chapter heading as "Guessing and Movement in
the Living Room." I left it in my hand and turned my
attention to the room in which I sat. It was an L written
deeply (with its thickness taken for its height) inside the
horizontal planes. The foot of this L was a little longer
horizontal planes. The foot of this L was a little longer
and wider than that of the usual one. From where I sat
and wider than that of the usual one. From where I sat
I could see only the point (area) at which the room
turned into this foot. I sensed warm pink and light yellow
reflections of the fading sun coming from around the
corner, from what I remembered to be substantial furni-
ture with bulging cushions. Only half of the large old-
fashioned globe was within my view. The door was in
full view a foot or two to the left of the globe. The longest
uninterrupted wall, the one from the heel of the L to the
head, the one along the left side of my view, was ribbed
with bookshelves. The most interesting books seemed
to be those farthest away.

———————— L ————— bay window.
——————————————————————————————
— — — — dozed — — — — — — — — — — —
——————————————————————————————
——————————————————————————————
— — — — — — — — eye — — — — eye — — — —
——————————————————————————————
— — — an eighth of a second — — — — — — —
——————————————————————————————
— — — — — to curb a certain degree of deviation,
— — — streets — — — — — — prose — — — — —
— — — — — — — vision — — — — — — — — —
— — — — walked — — — — — — — — — — —
— — — — — — — — cobblestone words — — — —
——————————————————————————————
——————————————————————————————
— — — — — — — — — somersaulted back to him.
On this page — — — — — — — — — — — —
——————————————————————————————
——————————————————————————————
— — — — drapes. — — — — — — — couch — —
——————————————————————————————
— — — — — — faucet running — — — — — — —
——————————————————————————————
——————————————————————————————
— — the water being squeaked off as the page ended.
"— — — — — —" — — — — — — erupted a burp.
——————————————————————————————
— — — — — — — — — shifting — — — — — — —
——————————————————————————————
——————————————————————————————
inclined plane — — — — — desk — — — — — lamp.

It was cloudy and it was getting dark enough to use it (a little), but I couldn't reach it without getting up off my seat so I decided not to for now. The sky was a chamber of clouds. Cloudy vapors dulled the window panes by padding them inside and out with their ropy gas fibers of an invisible weatherproofing substance. Grey and taupe vapors slapped the fresh air about.

I reassumed my position, curling up about myself in the chair. I twisted my back to rub my vertebrae to ease my back. Though I tried to have my weight become softly absorbed by the chair, I felt myself leaning heavily against it in eight separate places. Just before I began to continue to read, I released the paper to fall onto my lap and brought my hand up to touch my forehead. Then I brought it down to my eyes to ease the strain and then to my tongue which was moved to touch it.

When I looked down, the bold-faced print wavered up to me through the vague mist from the hollow of my lap.

The words on the page said: "Is there a postmark?" Guess. . . s or . o . Sunnypoint, Mass, Lapland, Stony-brook, Reading, Penn, Main, Oceanside, In Land Sound, Oak Land, Point Look Out, Hill Side, Lake View, Park Place, River Side, (2,7,3) Water Street, Valley Stream, Center Place, Lost Canyon, Meadow Brook, Under Cliff, Lake Wood, Green Street, Ridge Way, Point of Reference, Caesar's Ghost, Peach Pie!,!.

One short sniff was enough to assure me that the original author had had no part in this page. Instead the literal guest ballet of the microphy . . . Instead the frozen corps of the microphytic ballet . . . A microphytic colony had subsumed his role and imprinted itself on the page where it had become all stuck in its metaphors

Such an incident of light. A prosaic mosaic. The muscle tone of the entire page was misleading.

The stamp is a picture of a skeleton of a fish they said in a body. No, it isn't. Guess again. A worm's vagina, a speck of dust, a drop of dew, a cloud of hair, an underpinning, a broken wind, a loud spot, a tiny elephant, the tip of the deity's tongue, a cotton breath, a ticklish apostrophe, a valley of pimples, a wagonful of w's, a cause, gas gum, a mouse of gauze, a crumpled second, an o with an h, a twitch of glass, a side of a sneeze[n], a limp of desire, light on a table, o with r, a net made of butterflies, a grated speech, a talking pipette, siamese twin falcons, a talk, a cranky knot,[m] a mist of senses, a damper.

There was certainly no question about it. The smell was there certainly. It was surprising, though, that they were completely indiscernible to the touch. Touch. I let the page slip out of my hand not entirely sure that I had not been contaminated by the taut and tenacious microphytic agent. I nibbled on some crumbs from the tray and began to wonder what was holding up my host with my lunch. Is my sandwich ready, I said as I thumbed through the pages to find the appropriate one.

The sun poured onto my back and hugged my shoulders gently, almost at my skin scraping, loosely winding me about with light rays, stepping all over me, so much, much more so had it done so before so as it did not do so now with the grey and taupe vapors hanging around now mistily.

I took a sip of the pineapple juice. It was pineapple-grapefruit. The mist pinched the atmosphere. Moisture leaned up against me. It thus caused the curvilinear desire for something to drink to jut out just like that. The day continued.

The day continued without any refinements. Just like that, perhaps without any cause for alarm, the pineapple-grapefruit juice ran through me and touched just near bottom. It had become a nasty, cloudy day.

Tim lanced a boil on the lower calf of his right leg without so much as a murmur to alert the rest of the family. Gay carefully threaded the tape onto the machine and re-read the little note which her family (down in Aruba) had sent along with the recorded message to which they had devoted an entire afternoon. Mark pressed down hard with the orange rust crayon as he went over the outline for the third time. Lettitia told her daughter how pretty she thought she was. While the younger children huddled around a large armchair in the living room, Rhoda stood near the refrigerator as she put jelly on her slice of bread.

All this silence was leaving me with quite a mouthful. I was not using the benefit of my exercise. The tiny particles had been studying for thirty years the strenuous art of abstraction-deflection up to the point of a worded sentence. So that now the wordy tours jetés and minutely perfect extensions had come through practice to be a habit, a nearly natural function of the ropy gas shaving bodies to which they belonged. At times they even talked while unattended to. Here they were mumbling about how late the sandwich and how hungry I was.

The telephone was ringing off in the other room as I skipped the next page and went right onto the one which had the story of the first guess. A drop of mist had condensed just between the word "the" and the word "package." Water is magnetic in a special way. I think it is a choice melon was the first guess. Yellow? Green? Cantaloupe? I thought   ·

I thought Cantaloupe? Green? Yellow? I think it is a choice melon was the first guess. A drop of mist condensed just between the word "the" and the word "package." The telephone was ringing off in the other room as I skipped the next page and went right onto the one which had the story of the first guess.

Here they were mumbling about how late the sandwich and how hungry I was. At times they even talked while unattended to. So much for everything. So that now the wordy tours jetés and minutely perfect extensions had come through practice to be a habit of the ropy gas shaving bodies to which they belonged. The tiny particles had been studying for thirty years the strenuous art of abstraction-deflection up to the point of a worded sentence. I was not using the benefit of my exercise. All this silence was leaving me with quite a mouthful.

While the younger children huddled around a large armchair in the living room, Rhoda stood near the refrigerator as she put jelly on her slice of bread. Lettitia told her daughter how pretty she thought she was. Mark pressed down hard on the orange rust crayon as he went over the outline for the third time. Gay carefully threaded the tape into the machine and re-read the little note which her family (down in Aruba) had sent along with the recorded message to which they had devoted an entire afternoon. Tim lanced a boil on the lower calf of his right leg without so much as a murmur to alert the rest of the family.

It had become a nasty cloudy day. Just like that, perhaps without cause for alarm, the pineapple-grapefruit juice ran through me and touched just near bottom. The day continued with green outside and yellow inside. (?)

"Here's your sandwich," the man said as he put it down on the desk in front of me.

"Thank you."

I took a big bite of the crabmeat salad sandwich on white toast. The doorbell was ringing. The man rushed to the door motioning to me to just go right on with what I was doing.

"Mary Branerstein marries Mary Frank," I misread the first sentence on that page. The extruded words. Seated on the articulated banks of the stream of consciousness. A tall man walked into the room and sat down next to another man on the lap of the reader's cerebellum. Without a pause, a moment's hesitation, nothing could be seen. This time was a series of moments' hesitations. Through the crevice produced by an intention's subdivision comes the vision of the natural life abundantly supplied. So much can be said with only the [h] slightest effort. Suddenly Bea said, "Why not play the radio. There is no time to waste. I have a terrible cold. Do you have an extra tissue? What time is it? I can't stand the weather lately."

One day someone leaned way out, across, far across his dimly lit reaches, through the mist of the mist, through the convenience of life, on the [n] back of attention, along the path of an arm, by the pulse of a particularized place, just far enough out to touch the person next to him (who was there) saying: You are a waste product like me.

Co = conversation
S_1 = first speaker S_2 = second speaker
SW = spoken word

$$Co = (S_1 - SW) + (S_2 - SW)$$
$$Co = S_1 (1 - W) + S_2 (1 - W)$$

Tel. no. : 485-8295

SW = spoken word   W = written word   C = letters
N = sounds

$$SW = W - C + N$$

m = this letter was struck by accident

$$SW = Book - 4C + 3N$$
$$SW = Colder - 6C + 5N$$
$$SW = Imagination - 11C + 6N$$

As I started to read the third paragraph of page thirteen, I finished up the crabmeat salad sandwich which was good. Now I found myself reading word for word. The second line was about the nature of the logical guess. The third line was an extension of the premise of the first two. The fourth sentence had the words: seems, getting, to, be, quite, late. Although this sentence was necessary for the progress of the story, it tended to warp that particular paragraph out of shape. Then someone in the fifth line suggested that a thorough study should be made of the act of guessing. If a ratio could be found for the respective inputs of the logic of intuition, emotion and reason, for what would make up a good guess, it would be of tremendous importance. In the next line (in which?) he admitted that there would be a lot of guesswork involved.

The mist was almost dripping down as it snuggled about close and far. "Well as I live and breathe, if it isn't Ben's little boy Will you tell me i⸢   ⸣ht." "Step up and watch out for the doo⸢   ⸣ sense to it." "Without even asking m⸢   ⸣ "Right off the bat." "The law is the law." "I⸢   ⸣ that, homogeneous grouping is of course out of ⸢   ⸣ tion." "Stepping all over everything, not a care in mind." "About nothing." "Don't mention it." "The alarm clock didn't ring this morning." "Dont let a thing like that upset you." "Either you ʷᶠ have the knack for telling a joke or you don't." "And are you going to leave it just at that?" "That isn't it is underneath it."

I came from a small town on Long Island where the earth was fairly ᶠ fertile. Many little inlets let the water reach the potato and duck farms which circle the town. Mary came from a hill town rich with streams. Judy comes from some of the richest farmlands in this country.

The speaker was at the <u>rostrum</u> again. "Delicious, thank you," I screamed into the other room. As I paid attention in the direction of the kitchen, waiting patiently for my answer, I heard Will's mother explain how she would love to stay for Linda's party, but something, something, something, something and she'd be back for him at ——:30 or 7:00 at the latest.

I came down from the <u>rostrum</u> and walked back to my seat on the noduled <u>platform</u>. As I picked up the fourteenth page, the word and the blow came to me with ease. ~~Mary's guess, in a word, was pissmire colony. Why, because they had ordered them from California seventy-four years ago. And though the request had never been answered in her grandmother's lifetime, the receipt was still on hand. In fact, letters about the difficulties of procuring and then maintaining a healthy colony and the complications involved in the shipment of it were still part of their current affairs.~~

~~That was piss for urine and mire for ant, so named for their discharge, which was an irritant fluid so named because popularly regarded as urine.~~

The bottom corner of the package was already moist. Also, the lack of organization of the ant colony company would easily explain the absence of any marking on the package and the missing letter. By the end of the page, the others were mistily saying doubtful yet possible. Their guessing was startlingly interrupted by cries from outside.

Don't touch me. Stop it. I told you before. What! I don't care, leave if you want to. Don't leave. Don't touch me.

To describe how they'd reacted to this the author wrote: They felt the ^m centers of their feeling slip several vertebrae (or the equivalent distance but a little further within) down to a common level, a communal plane. This pulsating plane of anticipatory anxiety was like a firm, insubstantial trampoline off which, it was intimated to each and every one of them, each or every one of them could jump or spring with tremendous emotion at a moment's notice.

Speaking about <u>platforms</u>, in the almost physical sense I rested on at least three. There were, at least, the off-on-light-dark-nodular <u>platform</u>; the high-low, yes-no, etc., trampoline; and the <u>platform</u> for the bottom of the feet in the head. As much as these are all <u>platforms</u> in the almost physical sense, they are also other things. They will certainly be mentioned as what they are here as well as what they can or will to be even as they are what they are here. <u>PLATFORMS</u>, RESPITES, BRAIN PARTS, STRINGS, RECEIVERS, BUTTONS, TIPS, LIGHTS,[vs] FILTERS, BRANCHES, BOXES, FILTERS, HARD HESITATIONS, SOFTENED FIBERS, A PINCH IN THE CLOTH, FIELDS, A PINWHEEL OF PULSES, SOAKING WET SIGHT, SCRAMBLED EGGS, DIRTY EDGES, A FAUCET [h], LIGHT COFFEE (don't get off the track), THIRSTY WATER, WET BRAKES, TALKATIVE PLANTS, PROJECTORS or RUBBERY [n] LENSES or what you will. They [m] are substantially insubstantial. They are tenaciously inclined toward a solid, hard, hollow elastic pulpy quality. Through this inclination they undergo or come across everything indoors and outdoors, in every season, on the patio,[vf] in the library, etc., as for a start they pass through or come across friction, fluidity, liquefaction, lubrication, gaseity, vaporization, density, hardness, elasticity, texture, pulverulence, softness, water, air, ocean, land, gulf,[m] plain, lake, island, marsh, marsh, marsh, stream, wind, river, oil, resin, semi-liquidity, pulpy wads real or <u>wafted</u>.

Platforms can also be: G = grate or gas

R = rostrum or reason

A = attention or action

E = energy   T = time   B = bush

O = orbit

In this case a set (S) of platforms (p) would be:

Sp = G,R,E,T,A,G,A,R,B,O, — the name of a star.

Two people jumped up. They ran into each other, fell back and then righted themselves as best they could. They ran to the door and together pulled it open.

~~In the story, the two people saw their neighbor's wife (the one from the house on their left — south of them as their houses all faced west) scantily dressed beneath her navy blue raincoat or housecoat run~~ s ~~out of the house, through the spray of the all-night sprinkler, over the wet, slippery lawn to reach the sidewalk just as her husband opened the front door. As they watched, they also saw lights going on in three of the houses across the street (the one on the left — grey shingles with pink shutters; the middle one had a fieldstone façade with a special blue-plexiglass vestibule; the one on the right side — white shingles, blue shutters). They saw tele- phone wires with some birds on~~ n ~~them, part~~ s ~~of the moon, a chalky suggestion of the vanishing sun, spindly new trees, (don't skip the next one) street lights, gar- bage cans, some tiny children in the corner of the pic- ture running off out of view, a few passing cars, several parked ones including their own green Buick with one of the front doors not completely shut. They looked at these things and each preferred some to others even as they watched the outstanding events of the moment. They stood still and watched. They bounced with em- pathy on their neighborhood~~ vf ~~anxiety trampolines. Each had a universal and a particular one. They saw the woman now sensing her husband to be out of doors, behind her, dash into the street, wave down an oncom- ing car, jump in just in time and take off with the stranger (supposedly) just as her husband reached the street with a pair of her shoes in one hand and a small steak-knife in the other~~.

B.
More
or Later

MORE

When the speaker speaks at the <u>rostrum</u>, enunciated words are made to fly. They bounce off her, stream forward and fall back to her face and body. ~~She, of course, speaks from great convoluted depths no matter how shallow her puddle of thoughts. She wears nothing at first but usually succeeds in talking herself into a fairly convincing dressing gown.~~

A <u>quay</u> is a wharf usually made of concrete and stone. It is on the margin of a harbor or river, etc., alongside of which things are brought. It is obsolete to consider it the bank of a river or the shore of the sea. The reader's quay, the quay itself is constantly being firmly re-established even as it remains vaporous. But even the hardest substance has only as much body as a gas (or less) within the reader's point of view, so that the <u>quay</u> even as it remains vaporous might as well be concrete.

I sat in my host's library eating and reading, as the sun shone through and then didn't go on through the day, while others took walks, prepared meals, knitted and studied. I took long, measured strides along the ~~three-inch eye~~ walks of the page, which led me to the home of four people who lived in the country. The faucet was dripping in there. It was shut off. My stomach bothered me, so I burped and felt better.

Grey and taupe vapors composed a mist. As the grey mist swirled, for a moment, the taupe vapors were missed, until the grey parted and the taupe vapors strained themselves through. The sky, led through the end of the reader's line of sight (the quay), was seen as mist. Mist scene. The <u>quay</u> at the tip of the sighted pier hardened into a sighted touch of the body of mist which the reader saw. (?) My lips touched it too.

The mist was sighted. It has also been cited that hollow spaces contain many points of reference. The incidents of light have been noted and frequently reported.

I slipped out of my shoes. I put my finger through a hole in my stocking to scratch the calloused heel at least twenty times the day before when I had been doing something else.

The telephone was ringing in silence as it is doing now. There was so much exercise for nothing. Pineapple-grapefruit juice ran down with the words. So that now the wordy tours jetés, the wordy tours jetés . . .

Ropy gas fibers, ropy gas shavings, these are always present inside and outside. You can make wood shavings or shavings from a fruit. If a gas could have its outer edges gradually shaved off, if it were temporarily given the necessary solidity to allow this to be done while still remaining a gas, you could, as you have just done, in this way produce gas shavings. These would be of a ropy substance composed of stringy runners. These runners speed through a vapor as the agents of an intention. Once they have angled through it, they are brought into a new existence as the springy, pulpy substance of which their own growth has heralded the possibility. In this state, they carry messages, record actions, allow actions and when there is an intention provide runners. Similarly, when there are runners there are intentions. There will be more later.

I remembered the possibility of a ropy substance hardening into a pulp. Mary Branerstein was a series of moments' hesitations. The extruded words bunked into the chunks of melon as they fell through the gorge. Two individuals ran off the platform. The nodular platform was in this instance ribbed with bookshelves.

I didn't hear Judy bitterly complain that her having

had to prepare lunch for me had caused her to burn the birthday cake. Lovely Evelyn and Milton and Steve spent the night before there. Pearl came to visit and Lester met her there later. In, over, beside, next to, between, in front of, behind, through, by, with, for, up, to, against, under the mist, I was reading.

Not across a plain lake, a wooded field, a river stream, a windy hill, a gulf or a marsh but right out across her front lawn the woman ran clinging to her blue rain-coat. She ran through the word spray and touched its streams with her free hand. Around a motion's breeze spun a pinwheel of pulses.

These pages. Are they still touching?

The rostrum is in the hollow at the foot of the quay.
Say something.
Do you feel it?
It is as hard as a mosquito.
Step on it — <u>word</u>
The walking eye on a string
crosses the pier in sight
with calluses of color — grey, taupe, yellow
forming from the constant
friction with the mist.
It is in between.
Memory is made up of gas shavings.
These are possible, as is it,
only with a twist of the mind.
A platform is drawn up from thousands
of points of references.
They fold up and can be put completely away.
Sometimes these platforms on which the imagination
may rest or set up its rostrum
are completely reflecting

so that they become
a windy hill rich with streams
like the place which Mary came from.

LATER

I unfold a sentence. Out of the sphincter valve of each word comes the shorthand of a new sentence. And, here, in the defining mold which these sentences cast lies one flavor of my consciousness, perhaps vanilla.

Pearl (Kate,Judy,Ruth) came to visit and Lester (Maynard,Stephen,Allen) met her there later. Pearl is a woman's name. A woman is a human being with a vagina and breasts. A name is the way someone or something is called. A human is an animal which can recognize itself. Being is an alert substance (or a suggestion of this). Breasts are soft milky mounds. Everything is (was) substance. Soft is the quality which substance has of giving in (even if only a little) to a touch. As I am the only one who will read this, as I am reading it now, I declare subvocally these words as sentences: is, a, with, vagina, the, way, someone, something, called, an, which, recognize, itself, suggestion, of, this, milky, mounds, are, quality, has giving, in (in expresses inclusion with relation to space,place,time,state,circumstances,manner,quality,substance, a class, a whole, etc.) even, only, little, to, touch, everything, alert, etc., manner, circumstances, state, time, place, space, relation, inclusion, express.

Came indicates a move which has been made toward the speaker in some way in the past. Move is substance changing its place. Speaker is substance through which talk comes. I am forced to take these thoughts onto the next page where it is still raining.

Having moved across space, I have come to settle on the top, now leaving it, heading for the bottom of this page. The _past_ is the realm in which things have been changed. _Changing_ means that a substance (in varying degrees of organization) is not being what or the way it was. _Place_ is the consciousness' positioning of substance. _Talk_ is communicating sounds. _Realm_ is an area in time or space to which part of substance is relegated by the imagination. _Not_ in a word indicates a disappointment of the expectation of the imagination. These words have not yet been privately sentenced: been, made, comes, means, varying, degrees, organization, what, was, consciousness, positioning, communicating, sounds (the sentence of sound is to be the overflow or overreaching of movement), area, time, space, part, relegated, imagination, disappointment, expectation, overflow, overreaching.

The trial of the imagination ends in the sentencing of words. A list of things is a group of words. Words are made by: ink, print, paper, wood, air, electricity, light, holes, metal, glasses, rubber, erasers, smoke, lead, water, lemon juice, etc., tongues, connections, letters images, objects, films, nerves, blood, heat, fire, selection, decision, me and substance in every form.

Pearl came to visit and Lester met her there later. _To visit_ is to stay in place that isn't yours for a period of time. _To stay_ is to limit the area in which your particular movements take place. _Time_ is a platform (cf: this book). _And_ indicates that what comes after it is connected in some way with what went before. _Connection_ is the recognition of the intimacy of a division. _Recognition_ is to say that something is still similar to what it was. To make a _division_ is to give substance form. As I leave this paragraph, all the words which have not yet received some recognition (by means of underlining, sentencing, reiteration) follow and are now falling upon me: that,yours,period,limit,particular,take, after,went,before,intimacy,say,still,similar,give,form. I am telling you that you have been sentenced to see them move as raindrops do on a pane of glass.

This page is a continuance of my insertion. There is a word for this. It is, according to my preferences, a fecundating mathematical process, lubricated multiplication.

and Lester met her there later. Lester is a man's name. A man is an organization of highly formed substance with a penis. Organization is a collection and coordination of forms of substance and their movements for my amusement. Highly indicates here a substitution of degree of complication for a degree of vertical expansion. Coordination involves a recognition of a movement or its intention and an imitation of it or a move to supplement it and achieve a similar result. Substitution is changing the places of forms (words). I don't like to say this within your hearing since I do realize that though I am the only one reading this you will be sitting near me, holding the book for me and dividing my attention, but I must say that complication appears only in the confusion of the part viewing the whole, is the collision of all that is simple, and exists — again — purely for my amusement. I am asking you now to complicate this paragraph by simplifying the words which have not yet been recognized, by putting them into simple or complex sentences if you have the time which I give you.

I will find it perfectly acceptable to skip this page (cage,rage,age,sage), on which the end of the sentence and its multiplication are brought to a logical conclusion for the sole purpose of bringing them into existence in this place. <u>Met</u> is to have been (be) near the same place with someone or something and to have been aware of this. <u>Aware</u> is the particularizing of alertness. <u>Her</u> refers to a woman (or a thing which is referred to as one) who has been mentioned, pointed out or agreed on before. To <u>agree</u> is to coordinate results. <u>Later</u>, indicates that time has passed between the event referred to and what went before. I leave the unrecognized words to you. It is later now at the end of the sentence than it was at the beginning. Later, the end of the book will be later. It is always <u>later</u> than you think. This is due to the greasy long division of time and thought and action and time.

4.

The Body
of Letters
or
The Motion
of Words

The mist broke, the sun healed, the mist poured in, the sun sped out, lightning flashed, thunder thundered, the sun shone on a rainbow, the mist, lightning, flashing sun, blinding mist, taupe and grey rainbow, on the edge of the light, a drop of mist, a spot of sun, a barrage of light, an onslaught of vapors, a very shiny sun overcast with mist as forty-four million people (75% of these know C discovered Amer in the 13th century) moved. I read pages 15 to 26 which told the story of the murder of a moment along the subdued ridges of a crushed embankment of speech. The words clouded my eyes.

I appear on a page which would otherwise be blank. I, the mist, the agent, she, appear to swoop you and stratify you, circle you, and synthesize, just as I do now in this short paragraph into which I have fallen. I am not telling you but you are thinking that the two pages between which I fall were made by me in her for you to see you against the same word rain, through the mist, against different patterns of breath, similar but different accents to your attention. I have taught her how to make this special ruler by which you can measure yourself. In order to make the words move, you must give your attention to them. Notice I am gone.

The · mist · broke · the · sun · healed · the · mist · poured ·
in · the · sun · sped · out · lightning · flashed · thunder ·
thundered · the · sun · shone · on · a · rainbow · the · mist ·
lightning · flashing · sun · blinding · mist · taupe · and ·
grey · rainbow · on · the · edge · of · the · light · a · drop · of ·
mist · a · spot · of · sun · a · barrage · of · light · an ·
onslaught · of · vapors · a · very · shiny · sun · overcast ·
with · mist · as · forty-four · million · people · (75% · of ·
these · know · C · discovered · Amer · in · the · 13th ·
century) · moved · I · read · pages · 15 · to · 26 · which · told ·
the · story · of · the · murder · of · a · moment · along · the ·
subdued · ridges · of · a · crushed · embankment · of ·
speech · The · words · clouded · my · eyes ·

5.

Fog in the Tunnel
or
Intruding Words

In this case a good idea which I have given you is to do the opposite of what I say in spite of yourself: please don't touch the book and no kissing. Think of others before you think of yourself. Don't think of your family and the danger they are in at every moment. This is not the place for that. Perhaps the best way you could help me now would be to disappear. Vanish. Don't read the next paragraph on this page. Forget that you have ever seen this book. Scream for every word you will not see. Perceive nothing. Lose track of me. Kill me. And I hope that I am assured that you will not read between the lines.

I was falling. I fell thousands and thousands of miles in a sitting position until I reached the chair that I sat in and it touched my bottom. It was late afternoon. Most of the children had already arrived for the party in the other room.

I found the paper in front of me. I picked it up and started to read. I started at the limits set by the form of the letters and the outlines of groups of these, which turned into words. Each word that I knew had a finely balanced overall symmetry with which it had been endowed or which I had given to it as I had acquired it. The letters ^{vs} also had good balance. The curvature of the c, of the u, in the p and the a were unforgettable, as were the circularity of the o, the small e and the g. The others too were virtually indelible.

Through the curving lines rounded into words, the story twisted and twirled. It meandered directly to where it unfolded. Here an old ^{vf} man came into the room from behind them. He told them not to turn around. His face was disfigured. As he spoke the others twisted and warped their minds in an attempt to embody the distortion which was being presented to their backs.

I took a big breath and tried to straighten myself up in the chair, but this didn't help.

$$A = \text{Page } 59 \qquad B = \text{Page } 61$$
$$A = 4x - 8y - z = 0 \qquad B = x + 2y + 2z + 3 = 0$$

The back of the hand is resting on page 61 (B). The front of the hand is in the process of turning over (A). Find the angle (Theta) between the pages. Ans: Theta was 68 degrees.

Having eaten too much and too quickly and having engaged in only the most impalpable of exercises, I found myself under the weather, pouting as I picked up page thirty-two and brought it close to my eyes. I loosened my belt and my belly bulged out even farther. Opening the tin of Maalox and reaching for one with my bone-tired fingers, I saw the pill slip through my unbending fingers, pop onto the desk and off it to roll away down the left side of the room. It described a curvilinear path, maintaining a distance of three or four feet from the wall ribbed with bookshelves, and veered toward the right, toward the door in the wall opposite me. I took another. I roughly grabbed another and patted it onto my tongue. Chewing it to the grain, I then forced the pieces down with the back of my tongue.

The page was near me, on my fingers. As it was brought near me, to my face, it slipped between my dense fingers into a loose convex curve so that the words slipped out of sight near the bottom.

I bored into the story. The old man's acidic voice sliced through a great and chilling distance. As it delved into their ears, they summoned up their collective acuity to find him out. As they sucked in his monologue they tried to cut through to the revealing quaver and the whir in the hollow of his speech. They mined his voice; honeycombed his intelligence .

Despite the biting pain of the intrusion which nearly brought all listening to tears, each sharpened his wit, honing themselves one against the other; they attempted to force entry into the cavernous presence which addressed them from behind. They were alert to the possibility that his clipped tone, his biting inflection, his asymmetric phrasing might all be clues, perhaps even guidelines, to the nature and depth of his deformity.

I carefully extracted the next page from the pile of papers. I took a deep, deep breath, shut my lips firmly on it, exhaled through my nose, as, as, as at the same time that I was doing this, I was aware that I had begun to read. Words vaporized before my very eyes. My very eyes. As[s] I continued, they recondensed on the heavily padded internal tips of the line of sight. ~~These in turn moistened the lips of my imagination against which they pressed.~~ Foreign materials of every nature scraped against one another, absorbed one another. This brought to mind a strange coherence upon which the hope of my continuance depended.

The words informed me clearly but in muted tones. They whispered past my vision. In this way the sentences breezed in, almost catching me unaware.

They could almost hear the old man perspiring. He asked for some water. Through his mainly incoherent patter, it appeared that Mary was to bring it to him but with her eyes closed. Almost walking past him, she reached out and touched him. Her fingers became stuck in him. Horrified, Mary attempted to recoil. She was unable to release her fingers. It felt as though they were bound in a springy pudding. The old man hissed and wailed. About Mary's many fingers, the pudding pulsed warmly. Her eyes wouldn't open. Two noises began. They sent breezes, the winds,[n] storms, hurricanes of words, back and forth past each other's ears and under each other's noses. They blew each other up into a tornado[m] of screams. They did howl,roar,bellow as they yapped,grunted,yawled while they snorted, squeaked, neighed, cackled, buzzed, hooted, blattered, gobbled, lowed, pouted and clacked. Once Mary was pulled out of him, the old man's story ceased to be told behind them. He collapsed out of the room.

I sniffed the page.

As I picked up the next page, I was aware of the texture of the paper interposed between that of my fingers. Their structures were nearly aligned. The nap, tooth, web of the paper surface felt nice to the pulsing tissues of my fingers. It reminded me of the taste of mushrooms.

I looked down at the page. I saw its story through the brush of my eyelashes. The pill had eased my pain. I relaxed into the chair.

Each word on the page seemed ossified. The word face was a stone. The word guess was a flint. The words a, the, in, by, up, it, were pebbles. The word laughter was marble. Run was cartilage. Shelf was bone. Talk was an oak board. See was made of quartz. The word refrigerator was enameled. The word afternoon was concrete. The word iron was iron. The word help was wrought-iron. The word old was crag. The word touch was brick. The word read was mica and I was granite.

Every word is on the page. It has been read. Several other words came after the first group. Sentences depict lines. Each word is being read next to another being read. In time, the page will be read.

Words are water soluble. This is clearly and moistly so. After all the reader is a reef in the blue-eyed Red Sea. (And all this belongs to an organic question, it says.)

The whirlpool of the pivotal question subsides.
The mouth of the sea
Wet words peel off the surface tension
Screams of air bubble up

and mumble through
the clear embolisms of symbols

C = carbon   O = oxygen   U = uranium   G = gold
H = hydrogen   cough = COUGH

pH2ilOsOpHical investigatiOns

The gas mask reads in the mist $= 7 = 24$
Dream blood $= 2 = 10$
Word $= 1 = \ 4$
Instant water $= 2 = 12$

The honeycomb in the pulp
Pay cavernous attention
On a bone shelf
marble laughter
the teeth of the web
surfaced like paper in the wind
I was granite
then flint
The lowed cackle
of the michrophytic agent
perspires the silence

6.

A Type of Rainbow
or
By Order of Words

Words are moving over me. They fall through me and I hear that I am as tall as a tree. A straight line turns sharply into the corner of a rectangle. I watch lines of words fill in the diagonals. I am a precise cloud.

I am sure. Everything that is, is pulled toward me. Words selected at various degrees of discrimination must always discuss me even when I am semi-absent. The more words, the more combinations, the more portraits, the more negatives to be pushed away, the more positives on which to superimpose. I am so sure, aware, that there is not one word, aware, which can portray me. Instead every word, a confusion of words, may be used to surround me, to isolate me one foot above the page.

Every book fell through me. The way bubbles are held in soapy water, conversation is held in me, and when I blow, it is vocalized. I travel in words.

Read this aloud with your voice trailing your eyes: I am reading this aloud. Contrary to the 300 words per minute scan of the eyes, I progress nowhere, just quiver and nod.

I am the one who does not accept this sentence. I am reading in a circle. Now the word pencil is on the left side of the page. This sentence is going backwards. I am not reading this sentence, I am thinking of my family. I am dividing my ears from this voice so that I can hear it. I have turned the page without finishing this part. I am reading another page, not this. I am certainly doing what I am doing. I will not say that I don't know what I am doing, only that I can't say how I know.

I am warmer than paper. I can hold more words. My erasures can be made to reappear. Words need not merely press themselves parallel to me; any angle of entrance is acceptable and useful.

Draw a set of axes through the most central parts of your perception. If you don't feel it, make it arbitrarily, remembering that I will guide you. In terms of these, attempt to locate the combinations which the following words have ordered her to make.

Axis — the straight line, real or imaginary, passing through a body on which it revolves, or may be imagined to revolve.

Ball valve — a valve which works by the action of a ball resting on an inlet hole; pressure of the rising fluid raises the ball and opens the hole.

Change — to cause or turn to pass from one state to another; to vary in external form or in essence.

Nigh — (obs.) near to.

Mouth — the opening through which an animal takes in food; specifically, the cavity, or the entire structure, in the head of any of the higher animals which contains the teeth and tongue and through which sounds are uttered.

I — the person speaking or writing.

Motion — passage of a body from one place to another.

Read — to get the meaning of by interpreting its characters or signs.

Rummage — to search thoroughly and diligently, as through the contents of a receptable.

Direction — a directing; management.

Inenucleable — that cannot be removed without cutting.

Grease — the soft fat of game animals.

Leg — one of the supporting limbs in man or an animal, used in supporting the body and in walking and running.

Monsoon — any wind that reverses its direction seasonally or blows constantly between land and water.

The sun <u>rummaged</u> through the mist selecting material according to me. A petit <u>monsoon</u> occupied my platforms. And as several winds passed through my compartmentalized <u>mouth,</u> I tended to agree with them.

Words, sentences premeditated my spontaneous thoughtfulness. Stabilized by the thought of an <u>axis</u> to my thought, I <u>read</u> my mind with the page. I thought of a <u>ball</u> <u>valve</u> somewhere between the two. A ball is rising up from its resting place on an inlet hole as the fluid fills up the space appeared between the connecting lines.

I moved near to Mary's dying of <u>inenucleable</u> laughter. The jarring sound of it popped the probable face of the author into view. Then once again under his <u>direction</u> I conceived of the <u>change</u> that the amusing game had brought about in Mary. In fact, at this point none of them were as I had moments ago imagined them. Nor was the author's style any more what I had thought it was. He had been so taken with the laughter that he had remained doubled up, bent over with it in a corner of the last paragraph while the succeeding paragraphs were straining at the bit, or at any rate haphazard.

The page was brought to my nose. The smooth paper smelled only like the expectancy of a smell before a distinctive smell. In this case, there were obviously no bodies on the page. If the author were to claim an intrusion as an excuse for this page, in view of the findings of my nose, he would not have a <u>leg</u> to stand on. The joke about the 4^3 inch slab of <u>grease</u> with microphytic bacteria forming the most voluptuous of human lips was his baby.

Axis — the support for any rotating body, a shaft, axle or spindle.

Roric figures — figures exhibited by a polished surface when breathed upon under various conditions.

Foam — froth; spume; the substance which is formed on the surface of a liquid by fermentation or by violent shaking.

Change — variety.

I — an object shaped like an I.

Motion — the act of moving the body or any of its parts.

Between — an intermediate space, position or function.

Mouth — regarded as the organ of chewing or tasting; regarded as the organ of speech.

Read — to learn the true meaning of; to understand the nature or significance of as if by reading.

Valval — relating to a valve or to valves.

Direction — the address on a letter or a parcel.

Diplopia — double vision, appearance, of an object.

Grease — any thick oily substance or lubricant.

Leg — the part of a garment covering the leg.

Fiber — slender threadlike structure that combines with others to form animal or vegetable tissue.

Field — any wide, unbroken space.

I brought my hand up to my mouth and began to lick it, as was my habit. I stared down at the ink object shaped like an I which led me into the story of the man sitting directly to Mary's right.

Now I proceeded to read over his shoulder, to read _____* _____*

_____*

into that which the man was whispering to Mary. The undiagnosed illness of which he complained was, I felt sure, a severe case of diplopia. The probable cause was the inordinate amount of grease which a thorough examination had revealed to be present in both eyes. He did not say, but I feel sure that, as a matter of blurred fact, he rather enjoyed the constant change which this condition offered him. There is also, as might be imagined, a great delight to be had in seeing between an object and itself.

As for his philosophy, it is mine. The changes of the waft are not at all without a defining axis, a relative center. The axis, assured, might even be coordinated with a vital internal homologue, the spindle, that shaft about which my thought is spun and spinning. And this is the axis about which whirling fields (platforms) rotate past billions of fibers in the body of the imagination.

I read. My tongue slipped out of my mouth to lick my motionless hand. The legs of my slacks stuck to mine. The contrapuntal valval actions of my memory, my thoughts released a foam through which I perceived, now and then, roric figures mistily arranging themselves on a polished, rounded field of spun thought.

---

*This footnote is here to record a miracle. The asterisks above the line segments indicate the place at which three words appeared even before my fingers, my typewriter, arrived at that space on the paper. Neither the carbon paper nor the previous typewritten page proved to be the conveyor of these mysterious symbols which were lightly but legibly

Axis — the imaginary line passing through the center of a plane or solid; the central line with reference to which the parts are symmetrically arranged; any straight line for measurement or reference as in a graph.

Ligature — anything that ties or unites one thing to part of another.

Passible — that can feel or suffer.

Parallax — the apparent change in the position of an object resulting from the change in the direction or position from which it is viewed.

Change — a succession of one thing in the place of another.

I — symbol for iodine.

Motion — a meaningful movement of the hand.

Skatole — a foul-smelling crystalline substance produced by the decomposition of proteins.

Mouth — a person or animal regarded as a being needing food.

Read — to interpret as dreams, signs.

Cyst — any of certain saclike structures in plants or animals.

Osmotic — pertaining to or of the nature of osmosis.

Direction — instruction for doing, using, operating, preparing.

Grease — to cause to run smoothly.

Leg — anything that resembles a leg in shape or use.

Boomerang — something which recoils on whoever is using it or doing it.

---

printed there. Since these words seemed to coincide with what I'd been about to say, my first thought was that my thought had somehow managed to pre-empt the role of my hands and to outline itself there. After underlining and starring these, I went on with my writing. Later, looking up from the last paragraph, I found nine other words printed on that page. Now, at least, a discernible pattern made a small part of this strange occurrence clear. These specially selected words were light replicas of several of those which I had used to compose my story on that same page. With only a few exceptions they were printed from three to five lines below their twins. The words were: 1) which,

As I <u>directed</u> the centering <u>axis</u> of my being according to the cryptic instructions for my operations through at least three different platforms, levels, in a matter of ten minutes, the phenomenon of <u>parallax</u> took place somewhere between myself and the page in front of me. Within and without a pause there was always room for one thing in place of another.

An incorporeal <u>cyst</u> was formed to mark the occurrence of every <u>parallax</u> in my thought. The zone of incorporeal <u>cysts</u> within the field of my being, within the millions of fibers within the body of my imagination, was my memory. The intractable <u>ligature</u> between this memory zone of <u>cysts</u> and the various platforms of perception and interpretation was an a priori <u>osmotic</u> bond.

These delicate memory cysts would from time to time decompose releasing foul-smelling <u>skatole.</u> To prevent this from occurring too frequently, or for too prolonged a time, I used iodine, symbol <u>I</u>. I synthesized this, this <u>I</u>, through the grueling process of interpreting and reinterpreting dreams and signs and through squeezing the necessary tincture out of all this I <u>read</u>. I was vaguely aware that through all of this, I was designed to behave like a <u>boomerang</u>.

Once again the people in the story relaxed into the <u>greased</u> sequence which the author had thoughtfully provided for them. Every <u>mouth</u> had been filled. They were all <u>possible</u> on paper. The word chair had no <u>legs</u> and yet they were able to sit on it.

---

man, right; 2) the blur, much, 'tween, this(2), be, h(ad), cen(ter), There. A few possibilities: 1) This which he had there 'tween this man, this right center, much blur. 2) There be had much blur the 'tween this right man, this center. 3) Which man's right this blur much center be had there 'tween.

I love visitors, accidental mechanical ones, ghosts, microphytic agents, myself. I need this miraculous help as much as possible. In this book, I am the third I, near the beginning of a perhaps infinite series of them, and in the middle of this book.

More than inenucleable time on the mind
passing out roric figures
to grease the attention of the participators,
rummage through your intelligence, O Inenucleable
One. Forget the rostrum for the platform
and the platform for the field.
In there, cement is light.
Impossibly look for the points of reference
within the parallax.
It is so personal.
Don't forget the waft.
The spinning field makes it
and makes the calluses of color and form
as it rubs against, spins by the billions of fibers
and as it ends in a quay against the cemented sky.
Please grant this a priori osmotic bond forever.

7.

Dust Storm
or
The Pulverization
of the Metaphor

I will now squeeze through her vocal box. Set a high B pitch. Mmmmmn. If I give you a letter then you think of a word. I assure you that it will be the same word that I think of. Q — quay. Right. R — rostrum. Right. P — platform. Right.

I am made of an impossible cloth. (broth,sloth,moth) Listen to me. Now, right now. Whatever I say you must do. Anything I tell you, you will listen to. As I speak, so shall you move. Listen. Remember I have my claws of disease. I say to you now, Forget about these words. Throw them away. This one, right now. Out. Away. I am screaming at you. Don't listen to my words. Read this with your eyes (did you know that each of you have at least fifteen pairs) closed. I will tell you what you will do. I am telling you what you are doing. I am not writing this, I am talking it. Don't dare think otherwise. Are you listening to the razor in your ear? Put all thought out of your mind. Put it here . . . . Smell this sentence. Now do this. Cut off your head.

You better get away from yourself for awhile. Burn these words with your attention but do not see them. Metaphors wind like country lanes swerving by bushes, children, horses, streams, waterfalls, ants, tigers, penguins, fingers, breakfasts, atoms, skies, windows, ostriches and orchards. I plant these in my soil. I transplant these to grow in my soil.

I have your head over here. Come here and get it. I will let you feel it again. Here are the wet, deep tube, the powdered face, the light-sensitized almonds, my ear drums, the balanced parts whose normal composure is arrived at by my telling you so. Try not to look at your nose, pick me up off this page again. There must be a strong concentration of me in you.

The mist removed itself from my presence. The sun came in the window. It went over the rills of my shoulders as I leaned my head and then my imagination back into it a little (40 degrees).

Up until entrance into the lives of the characters after their departure from the typewriter carriage, I was moving about in my chair, trying to get into a more comfortable position.

There were many different movements on that page. No one seemed to get confused. Mary walked over to the window. One of the men began to talk without stopping. This made it difficult but not impossible for the author to intertwine and then present the action of the others. Their movements radiated from the tips of his fingers. Someone else opened the newspaper and started to read. The old man's intrusion was not discussed. Two of the people were whispering in the corner.

The shine of the sun particularly illuminated the foot of the y in Mary and the word newspaper. I peeked through my eyes. A sentence was appearing. There was a sentence. I read it up. It disappeared in the reading. It disappeared just in time to escape the superimposition of the next one. A sentence. It hung on the words of the last one.

The sentences linked arms (as the words did sinews) as they vanished from this earth. Only a bit of grit of the words remained. This brought out the quality of the imagination as salt or accent does to a thick steak. The sentences made impressions in millimeters.

The draft settled on my crinkled face. I resumed the swallowing of the dream. I kicked aside the rostrum with a shred of my foot as it peeled off my mumbled throat. Large agonies flew by me. I was balancing on top of a volcano immersed in my reading.

Three platforms. Now it was a question of at least six. There were the feet in the head; there was .... and ....; one platform had boards made of radios nailed into place with gaseous antennas; another was a beaded ocean's surface; there was an enormous .... as a word wrapped tightly in letters fell onto the .... I turned from platform to platform dividing my time. I slipped right through my middle; I waded; I flew; I rubbed up against myself; I stood up; scraped, beamed, scraped, beamed, clasped, numbed, clasped numbed; severally glistened, sawed, torched, toasted, smiled.

My Grecian eyes, the eyes from before Christ, dovetailed to the page. They met each other in the middle. The segmentation of the page parted their memory. Ropy gas fibers bulged inside as the counterparts of the opened spaces. I adjusted my softness. I allowed for my head or its environs to be broken, as though the wet air between my temples (saffron robes, franciscan cloaks, pressed rosemary, tifillen seen from around the corner), cracks parted, fissures steamed, the incision of the words was effected. Ten parts of me supported the maintenance of my opened upper eyelids. Passions lined up to be felt. Tired rhythms, a usual part of the decisive normal temperature's echoing space, hummed an attentive fugue. On this came to rest the peal of the isolated page, the tone of words, a tuneful air, sound selections of the author, microphytic movements.

I was reading. I swallowed the ropy gas fibers. The most significant thing I was doing was creating a platform, perpendicular to my forehead, parallel to the sentences.

With excruciating ease, I was reading. I was peeking out. I was reciting to myself before stepping up to the rostrum. I was walking and talking. In other words, in many other words: ~~I was turning a crank, socializing, of course; I was cooking in a pot on my neck the stove which used the same device as a timer and a furnace, I was drinking and extracting, I was~~ STRETCHING, CHEWING, RUNNING, LEAPING, SMOKING, PICKLING, FORTUNE TELLING, ASKING,[vs] ANSWERING, STEPPING, SLEEPING, OPENING, CREASING, ARRANGING, PACKING, STUFFING, FILLING, PILING UP, FILING, SENSING, SAWING, SCRATCHING, WAITING, SPENDING, FISHING, CRACKING, TOUCHING, BORROWING, SUPPORTING,[vf] COUNTING, LOSING, FINDING, MIXING, TRYING (I had had years of practice), MAKING, DRILLING, TURNING, SOFTENING, LYING, SUMMONING, DELIVERING, STEPPING, BOUNCING,[s] HOPPING, SKIPPING, JUMPING UP OUT OF AN ENTRENCHMENT, FLOATING, SPINNING, LANCING, TRAINING, PASTING, STAMPING, WRAPPING, TYING, BALANCING, FEELING, LICKING, MOLDING, MOULDING, WRITING (WITH A BLOOD VESSEL STYLOS), GORGING, RELEASING (SHORT-LIVED BALLOONS OF IMPRESSIONS) AND APPENDING.

Another list might be made of what I was undergoing. In any case I was certainly (this word certainly is meant to feel like you feel when you pull on a sturdy piece of thread which is attached to something you don't see; this thread is not going to snap) caught on the hook at the end of the author's line.

The comfortable position
is felt in the sinews
hung on words
with excruciating ease
Millimeter impressions
pressed outside out
spinning and cracking
Making a stuffing
Molding a moulding
and ballooning
into something sturdy
which will usually not snap.
Two of the people were whispering
in the corner

8.

Lightning
or
The Wording of
the Reader

I've read enough. I'll read more. I held the manuscript in my hand. I shook it. Not a word came out. I put the pages back down on the desk, ~~the polished smooth desk.~~ My head fell into my hands. I opened my eyes. Not a word fell out. I forced air out of my nose to clear the passage. The weather creaked through my bones.

I've read enough. I'll read more. I read "The Atlantic Ocean" on the half of the globe still in view. Floor, brown; desk, brown polished wood; bookshelves, wood color; books, bound with lacquered paper, some leather. I saw the floor extend to the door. The floor and wall, with the space combined with the door, led me to construe that it was partially open. The door itself was not open.

— — — — — — — — — — — — early part of — —
— — — — — — — — Mary — — — — — — — thought
— — — — — — — — — — — — — several legs — — —
— — — — — — — the height of the — — — — — — —
— —
— —
— — — — — — doubled and upside down — — — —
— — — — very high gloss. — — — — — — — — —
— — — — — — — — — — — — — —

I went fast. Faster than I have ever done before. I was picking up the meaning without stopping to accumulate words. Speed. I loved it. Soon it would be over. The words stuck to the mist, I to the meaning.

My hat; did I bring it with me? Where. Yes, I came in with it. It's on the table. The table in the corner. My hat is on the table in the other part of this L-shaped room, ~~the part I can't see.~~

~~The mist dappled my face.~~ I settled down in my body. The mist was settling down too. The smell of fragile birthday candles (blue, I thought) being snuffed out, wove in through the partially opened door. Another smell straddled it grotesquely. The microphytic agent? Who asked that. The mist steamed out the two o's of my nose. That's impossible.

I poured my concentration down onto the page. I thought the word "parallel" was mispelled. Only half of me knew how to spell. I concentrated on it, but I was no longer on sure grounds.

— — — — — — — — beaver — — — — — — —
— — — — pies — — — — — — — up the last end — —
— —
— — sure enough — — — — — — surprised — — — —
— — — — — — — emulsified wish — — — — — — —
— — — — — — — — — — — — — paralll — — — — — —
— — — — — tongue dry — — — — — — — — — —
— — — — — — — kept — — — — — —

I was manipulating space; I was hammering dreams; I was bathing; I was reading soap; I was running and falling and washing off my knees with the word soap; I was truly whiling away my time and dividing my attention.

— — — — — — was moist — — — — — — — —
— —
— — — — —.
— — — — — — — — — — — — — — — — — — —
— — — — — — — — — — — — — — living proof — — —
— —
— — shivers — — — — — — embedded — — — — — —
— — — — — — — — — — — — stepping — — — — —
without having been — — — — — — — — — — — —
— — — — — — — — surfaced — — — — —.

How many more pages. How much more? I kept on reading as I felt the pile to go. Twenty or thirty pages, no years. The mist punctuated my face. It underlined the bags of my eyes. It rained through my eyelashes. It met with the perspiration on my blouse. In my nose, there was a smell. I held my nose. I adjusted my body. I stared with a pair of wide-opened eyes at page fifty. I stepped on my foot to wake it up. But my words meant nothing to it. My eyes jerked closed. In this way, I read my copy of page fifty correct in every detail. As page fifty slipped down through my neck (it had to roll itself up to do this), slipped into my chest, rested there awhile touching my shoulders just a little bit away from their rounded ends and then down to my stomach to be supported from below by the hip bones, I read the next page which I'd never seen, with my eyes still closed. It was very difficult and went very slowly. When I was finished I took up page fifty-one and read through once quickly. In both cases, the story had been propelled forward, but I, I had escaped his syntax despite our mutual dependence on the logical connectives. However both pages had microphytic the odor of microphytic spelling inside and out.

— — — — — — — peeling rain — — — — — — — —
— — — — — — — — — — — — — — — — — — — —
— — — — — — — — — — savage glass — — — — — —
— — — — — — — — — — — — — — — — — — — —
— — — — — refilled the purple stump — — — — — —
— — — — — — — — — — — — dry anticipation.
— — — — — — — — — — — — — — — — — — — —
— — — — — — streaming — — — — — — — — — —
— — — — — — — — — — — — — — — — — — — —
— — — — — — — — — — — — — — — — — — — —
— — — — — — — — — — — — — — — — — — — —

— — — — — — — — — — — — — —
— — — — — — — — — — — — — —
— — — — — — — — — just couldn't stop it — — — —
— — — — — — — — — — — — — —
— — — — — — — — — — — — — —
— — — — — — — — in the midst of — — — — — — — — —
— — — — — — — — — changing — — — — — — — —
— — — — — — — — — — — — — —
— — — — — — — — near.
— — — — — — — — — — — — — —
— — — — — — — — — — — — — —
— — — — — — — — — — — — — —
— — — — bottom fell out — — — — — — — — — —
— — — — — — — — — — — — — —
— — — — — — — — — — — — — —
— — — — — — — — — on a platform, but not just an
ordinary — — — — — — — — — — — — — —
— — — — — — — — — — — — — —
— — — — — — — — — — — — — —
— — — — — — — wide-angle — — — — — — —
another present — — — — — — — — — — —
— — — — — — — — — — — — — —
— — — — — — — — — — standard — — — — —
— — — — — — — — body cloth.
— — — — — — — — — straighten it out. — — — —
— — — — — — — — — — — — — —
— — — — — — — — — — — — — —
for me — — — — — — — — — — — — —
— — — — — — all the nerve — — — — — — —
— — — — — — — — — — — — — —
burnt — — — — — — — transpiration — — — — —
— — — — — — — — — — — — — —
— — — — — — — — — — — — — slowly — —
— — — — — — turned up — — — —.

— — — — — — the soaking issue — — — — — —

— — — — — — — — — — — — — — — — — — —
— — — — — — — — — — — — — — — — — — —
— — — — — — — — — — — — — — — — — — —
— — — — — — — — — — — — — — — — — — —

— — — — — — colder and darker between the self-
repelling like poles of the mist poultice — — — — — —

— — — — — — — — — — — — — — — — — — —
— — — — — — — — — — — — — — — — — — —
— — — — — — — — — — — — — — — — — — —

— — — — — — sensitive material — — — — — —

— — — — — — — — — — — — — — — — — — —
— — — — — — .

— — — — — — — — — — — — — — — — — — —

boil — — — — — — — — — — — — — — — — —
— — — — — — — — — — moving — — — — — —
— — — — — of course — — — — — — — — — —
— — — — — — — — — — — — — — — — — — —

— — — — — — — — — — — — rid it of that strange
oily smell — — — — — — — — — — — — — — —

— — — — — — — — — — — — — — — — — — —
— — — — — — — — — .

— — — — — — — — — — — — — — — — — — —
— — — — — — — — — — — — — — — — — — —

within hearing — — — — — — — — — — — — —
— — — — — — — — time line — — — — — — —
— — — — — — — — — — — — — — — — — — —
— — — — — — — — — — — — — — — — — — —
— — — — — — — — — — — — — — — — — — —

— — — whose attitude — — — — — — — — — —
— — — — — — — — — — — — — — — — — — —
— — — — — — — — — — — — — — — — — — —
— — — — — — — — — — up — — — — — — — —
— — — — — — but buttressed — — — — — — — .

— — — — — — — emerging — — — — — — — —
— — — — — — — — — — — — — — — — — — —
— — — — — — — — — — — — — — — — — — —
— — — — — — — — — — — — — — — — — — —
— — — — — — — — — — — — — because — — — — —
— — — — — — — — — — — — — — — — — — —
— — — — — — — — — — — — — — — — — — —
— — — — — — — — — — — — — — — — — — —
— — — — — — — splashing with guttural shrieks for
accompaniment. — — — — — — — — — — — — —
— — — — — — — — — — — — — — — — — — —
— — — — — — — — — — — — — — — — — — —
— — — — — — — — — — — — — — — — — — —
— — — — — — — soaking — — — — — —.
— — — — — — — — — — — — — — — — — — —
— — — — — — — — — — — — — — — — — — —
— — — — — — — — — — — — — — — — — — —
— — — — — — — on, still touching the craggy inner
facing — — — — — — — — — — — — — — — —
— — — — — — — — — — — — — — — — — — —
— — — — —.
— — — — — — — — — — — — — — — — — — —
— — — — — up from below — — — — — — — — —
— — — — — — — — — — — — — — — — — — —
— — — — — — — — — — — — — — — — — — —
— — — — — — — — — — — — — — — — — — —
— — — — — — — — — — — — — — — — — — —
— — — — Idlewild — — — — — — — with the taxi strike
— — — — — — — — — — — — — — — — — — —
— — — — — — — — — — felt I'd rather finish now — —
— — — — — — — — — — — — — — — — — — —
— — — — — — staying then. I'm going — — — — — —
— — — — — — — crystal bedrock — — — — — words.

———————— wet assault —————————

——————————————————————————

——————————————————————————

——————————————————————————

——————————————————————————

——————————————————————————

————————— still here ————————————

——————————————————————————

——————————————————————————

————— .

——————————————————————————

——————————————————————————

——————————————————————————

——————————————————————————

——————————————————————————

————— cooking and went to take it out ————

——————————————————————————

——————————————————————————

——————————————————————————

——————————————————————————

——————————————————————————

———— completely forgot ————————— an article

——————————————————————————

—————————————————————————— .

——————————————————————————

——————————————————————————

————————— .

——————————————————————————

——————————————— parched ridge ————

— — — — — drew it off of — — — — — — — — — — —
— —
— — — — — — — — — — — — — — — — — never — — —
— —
too —
— —
— —
— — — — — — — I was still aware — — — — — — — —
— — — — — — — — — — — — which was certainly a
possibility — — — — — — — — — — — — — — — — —
— — — — — — — — — — — having accepted — — —
— —
how thoughtless of me. — — — — — — — — — — — —
— —
— — — — — .

— — — — — — — — — — — — — — — — — — — —
of —
for —
still —
— —
— — — — — — — glass from the table — — — — — —
— —
and — — — — — — — the curtain aside — — — — —
— —
— —
They'd never felt more — — — — — — — — — — — —
— — — — — — — — — — — — — — — a moving moment
— —
— —
though the refrigerator door had been left open and —
— —
— —
— — — — — — — — .
— — — — — — — dry corner.

I crossed the waves of — — — — — countenance. I returned to my cave in the midst of the mist. When I had started, I had had carved and shiny words and paragraphs of sentences strung out as far as the eye could see. Once inside, I found only grit and dust. — — — — — — — — — against which the mist scratched — — — — — — — — — —. The same things which I had had to be careful not to get into my eye. Yet minutes later, I found that as usual when I allowed their weight to lean on me, to scratch me, they haunted me with the ghosts of the worded page. — — — — — — — — — — — — — —
— — — — — — — — — — — — — — — — —
— — — — — — — — — — — — — — — — —
— — — — — — — — — — — — — — — — — and if they scratched for too long they would begin to tickle and make me laugh.

Over in the corner of the story, the whispers were now nearly audible.

"— — me, that — — — — — how — — — I know?"
"Of — — — — — — — — its prerogative."
"— — — — — — — question, — — that?"
"And — — — — not?"
"— — — — — — the — — — — — — you."
"If — — — — — — — — — — — blush to — —
— — — —. — — — — before — — — — — — or
— — — — — — — — — — — — have taken."
"— — — — — — — — — — — — decided?"
"— — — — — — — — — — — — — — —"
"With — — — — — it is, — — — — — — — —
— — — — — — — — —"

"Groundless."

The children seemed to be enjoying the party at the other end of the apartment. I'll just finish this chapter, I mentioned.

— — — — — — — — — — — — — — — — — —
— — — pulsing magnetic calvacade dripping — — —
— — — — — — — — — — — — — — — — — —
— — — — — — — — — — — — — — — — — —
— — — — — — — — — — — — — — — — — —
— — — — — — — — — — — — — — — — — —
— — — — — — — — — — — — — — — — — —
— — — — — — — — — — — — — — — — — —
— — — — — — — —.

I turned my head around toward the window which
opened up the startingly cold afternoon to me. I turned
back to the desk and the waiting page. The page kept
reimbursing my eye-clogged eyes for the incorporeal,
immaterially small deposits as I hastened along with
them and the other things which I had at my disposal
at that moment. I was in a hurry to get to the finishing
line, find the point, find out what it was about and close
the manuscript back between its covers. — — — — —
— — — — — — — — — — — — — — — — — —
— — — — — — — — — — — — — — — — — —
— — — — — —.

— — — — — — — — — — — — — — — —
— — — — — — — — — — — — — — — — — —
— — — — — — — — — — — — — — — — — —
— — — — — — — — — — — — — — — — — —
typed in — — — — translucent façade — — — — — —
— — — — — — — — — — — — — — — — — —
— — — — — — — — — — — — — — — — — —
— — — — — — — — — — — were characterized — —
— — — — — — — — — — — — — — — — — —
— — — — — — climbing rather than walking — — —
— — — — — — — — — — — — — — — — — —
— — — — — — — — — — — — — — — — — —
— — — — — — — craggy rim — — — — — —.

———————————— somersaulting and splashed
the page with ——————————————————
——————————————————————————
——————————————————————————
with the approved proposal for a new system of wiring
——————————————————————————
——————————————————————————
——————————————————————————
I stretched ——————————————.
——————————————————————————
——————————————————————————
——— package from view ————————————
——————————————————————————
———————————— in the telling ——————————
——————————————————————————
rested on the inertia of his impulse ————————————
————————— but was lying there awake ————
—————————.
——————————————————————————
———————————— closing paragraphs ——————————
——————————————————————————
——————————————————————————
————————————————— delicate and fine ————
——————————————————————————
—————— memory ————————————————
————————————— v ———, p ———, m ————,
e ———,——————————————————————
——————————————————————————
——————————————————————————
——————————————————————————
——————————————————————————
rubbed ——————————————————————
———————— substantially obscured ——————————
—————————.

— — — — questions came pouring — — — — — —
— — — — — — — — — — — — — — — — — — —
— — — — — — — — — — — — — — — — — — —
— — — — — — — — — — — — — — — would give — —
— — — — — — — — — — — — — — — — — — —
— — — — — — — — — — — — — — — — — — —
— — — — — — — — — — — — — — — — — — —
— — — — — — — — — — — — — — — — — — —
— — — — — — — — — — — — — — — — — — —
well — — — — — — — — — — — — — — — — — —
— — — — — — — — —.

— — — — — — — — — — —
"What was that sound? — — — — — — — — —"
— — — — — — subject — — — — — — — — — —
— — · — article — — — — verb adverb — — — — —
— — — — — — — — — —. Subject verb adverb article
adjective noun conjunction article adjective adjective
noun. — — — — — — — — — — — — — — — —
— — — — — — — — — — — — — — — — — — —
— — — — — — — — — — — — — — — — — — —
— — — — — — — — — — — — — — — — — — —
— — — — — — — — — — — — — — — — — — —
— — — — — — — — — — — — — — — — — — —
— — — — — — — — — — — — — — — — — — —
— — — — — — — — — — — — — — — — — — —
— — — it just needs a little rest — — — — — — — —
— — — — — — — — — — — — — — —. — — —
— — — — — — — — — — — — — — —.
— — — — — — — — — — — — — — — — —
— — — — — — — — — — — — — — — — — —
— — — — — — — — — — — — —. — — — — —
— — — from the morning — — — — — — — — —
— — — — — — — — — — — — —. — — — — —
— — — — — tight water tight — — — — — —.

— — — — — fluid thrust — — — — — — — — — — — —
— —
— —
— —
— —
— —
— — — — — — just letters — — — — — — — — — —
— —
— —
— — — — — — — — state of mind.
— —
— —
— —
— —
— —
— —
— — — — — — — — touching — — — — — — — — —
— —
— —
— — — — — — — —.

I didn't bother to pick up the few pages that had slipped out of my hands and fallen onto the floor beneath the desk. Instead I remained deeply engrossed in page 83 which buckled and bulged with the wild animal thoughts, the supposedly simply phrased thoughts of the once equally engrossed author which — — — —
— —
— —
— —
— — deceptively — — — — plain printed page before
— — — — — — — —.
— — — — — — — — — dam — — — — — — — — —
— —.

— — — — — — — trickling influence — — — — —

— — — — — — — — — — — — — — — — — — —

— — — — — — — — — — — in passing — — — —

— — — — — — — — — — — — — — — — — — —

— — — — — — — — — — — — — — — — — — —

was astounded — — — — — — — — — — — — — —

— — — — — — — — — — — I tried to remain — — —

— — — — — — — — — — — — — — — — — — —

— — — — — — — — — — .

— — — — — — — — — — — — — — — — — —

— — — — — — — — — — — — — — — — — — —

— — — — — — — — — — — with not a hair out of

place — — — — — — — — — — — — — — — — —

— — — — — — — — — — — — — — — — — — —

— — — — — — — — — — — — — — — — — —

poured over it — — — — — — — — — — — — —

— — — — — — — — — — — — — — — — — —

— — — — — — — — — — — — — jumping all over

the page in her printed dress — — — — — — — — —

— — — — — — — — — — — — — — — — — —

— — — — — — .

— — — — — — — — — — — — — — — — — —

— — — — — — — — — — — — — — — — — —

— — — — — — — my own feeling — — — — — —

— — — — — — — — — — — — — — — — — —

— — — — — — — — — — — — — — — — — —

— — — — — — — — — — — — — — — — — —

— — — it functioned as a — — — for the — — — which —

— — — — and sparkled with — — — — — — — — —

— — — — — even now as they prepared to undo — —

— — — — — — — — — — — — — pieced together

— — — — — — — — — — — — — — — — — —

— — — — — — — — — — on edge — — — — — —

— — — — — — — — — — — .

— — — Gothic rain — — — — — — — — — — — — —

— — — — — — — — — — Memphis — — — — — — — —

— —

— —

— —

— — — — — pummeling new tongue born — — —

— —

— —

— —

— — — — — — — — — — — — — — — —.

— — — — — with naval jelly dematerializing — —

— —

— —

— —

— — — — — — — — — — — — — loosely — — — — —

— — — placed in the imagination — — — — — — —

— —

— —

— —

— —

— — — — — — — horizontal dragging presence with

its — — — — — — — — — — — — — — — — — — —

— —

— —

— —

was approached — — — — — — — — — — — — — —

— —

— —

— — — — — — — touch in every sense — — — — —

— — — — — — — —.

— —

— — — — — — — — — — — — reader wind — — —

— —

— — — — — — — — — still rigid ledge — — — —.

———————————————— man's head cast —
——————————————————————
—————————————— letter ————
——————————————————————
——————————.

——————————————————————
————————————————— "purpose" —
——————————————————————
caught "purpose" —————————— pale ——
——————————————————————
——————————————————————
——————————————————————
——————— had been delayed.
——————————————————————
——————————————————————
———— to face me. ———————————
——————————————————————
——————————————————————
——————————————————————
——————————————————————
———— weight ——————————— the scale.
——————————————————————
——————————————————————
—————— unforgettable —————————
——————————————————————
——————————————————————
——————————————————————
————— stopping material —————————
——————————————————————
——————————————————————
———— his density ——————————————
——————————————————————
———————— splattered ——————————
define ————.

— — — — — — — — — moist emittance — — —
— — — — — — — — — — — — — — — — — —
— — — — — — — — — — — — — — — — — —
— — — — — — — — — — — — — — — — — —
— — — — — — — — — — — — — — — — — —
— — — — — up the pick — — — — — — — — —
— — — — — — — — — — — — — — — — — —
— — — — — — — — — — — — — looseleaf — — —
— — — — — — — — — — — — — — — — — —
— — — — — — — — — — — — — — — — — —
— — — — — — — — — — — — — — — — — —
— — — — — pound with — — — — — — — — —
— — — — — — — — — — — — — — — — — —
solid limbs — — — — — — — — — — — — — —
— — — — — — — — — — — — — — — — — —
— — — — — — — — revealing curtain — — — — —
— — — .
　　— — — — — — — — — — — — — — — — —
　　— — — — — — — — — — — — — — — — —
　　— — — — — — — — — — — — — — — — —
　　— — — — — — — — — — — — — — — — —
— — — — — — — — — — carbon shadow — —
— — — remembering to take stock — — — — — — —
— — — — — — — — — — — — — — — — — —
— — — — — — — — — — — — — — — — — —
— — — — — — — — — — — — — — — — — —
— — — — — — — — — — — — — — — — — —
seventy-eight words — — — — — — — — — — —
— — — — — — — — — — — — .
　　— — — — — — — — — — — — — — — — —
— — — — — — — — — — — — — — — — — —
— — — — — — — — — — — — — — — — — —
— — — — — — — — — — — — — — — — — —
— — — sturdy, narrow rise, still here, still dry — — — —.

——————————— within the continuous stream
to the point of saturation — — — — — — — — — — —
— — — — — — — — — — — — — — — — — — — —
— — — — — — — — — — — — — — — — — — —
— — — — — — — — — — — — — — — — — — —
— — — — I wiped off my face with my hands of — — —
— — — — — — — — — — — — — — — — — — —
— — — — — — — — — — — — — — — — — — —
— — — — — — — — — — — — — — — — — — —
— — — — — — — — — — — — — — — — — — —
I wasn't tired in fact I wasn't — — — — — — — — —
— — — — — — — — — — — — — — — — — — —
— — — — — — — — — — — — — — — — — — —
— — — — — — — — — — — — — .
— — — — — — — — — — — — — — — — — —
— — — — — — — — — — — — — — — — — —
— — — — — — — — — — — — — — — — — —
— — — — — — — — — — — — — — — — — — —
printed facing — — — — — — — — — — — — — — —
— — — — — — — — — — — — — — — — — — —
— — — — — — — — — — — — — — — — — — —
— — — — — — — the others walked out after her — —
— — — — — — — — — — — — — — — — — — —
— — — — — — — — — — — — — — — — — — —
— — — — — — — — — — — — — — — — — — —
— — — — — — — — — — — — — — — — — — —
— — — — — — — — — — — — — — — — — — —
— — — — — — — — — — — — — — — — — — —
— — — slapped it closed, the dust breath — — — — —
— — — — — jumped — — — — — — — — — — —
— — — — — — — — — — — — — — — — — — —
— — — — — sudden parchment — — — — — — — —
— — — — — — — one drop — — — — — — — —
— — — — — — narrow rise — — — — — — — —

She is raining
Moving a sensitive material
Soaking the craggy inner facing
It wasn't missed
The looseleaf body cloth
strung on solid limbs
Prints its address
with such a touching sight
dragging its presence horizontally
ounces of carbon shadow
before eyefall
a drying glove between the inside
and the outside hand in mist
just letters.
Headwinds and a light rain.

9.

A.

Mist and Flood
Evaporating Endings

B.

Condensation
The Reader and
the Weather

i entered the m(i)st. i started (i)odine. i filled f(i)ll. i make h(i)m. i am always (i)n. (So what)

I have spoken loudly at the <u>rostrum.</u> I have stood on three or more <u>platforms.</u> I spoke loudly, enunciating clearly, wide and sharply, my words have flown wide of the paragraph, out of the head, into rivers, onto desks, down tubes, down into mines and caves, up to those tiny, brilliant dots larger than I suppose (calling them stars), up into space, down to say sky. They've fallen onto dogs, birds, turtles, fish, tops (spin), spoons, plates, windows, cars, matches, sofas, chairs, beds, towels (this one is dry), subways, buses, tables, lamps, hands, eyes. They've tumbled and squeezed through, at the last moment, strings, juices, threads, hairs, tendrils, wax, printed matter, sacs, canals, ducts, bones, labyrinths, membranes, twigs, nerves, spiral ligaments, two minute muscles — stapedial and tensor tympani, floors and walls, living cloth stretched over fossilized cartilage, the ears and skulls.

— — — — — — wet spot — -- — — — — — — — — — —
— —
— —
— — — — — — — — — — — rib cage — — — — — — —
— —— — —
— — — — — — — — — — — — — — — — — — —— — — —
— — — — — — rough — — — — — — — — — — — —
— —
— — — — — — — — — — — — — —- — — — — — — —— —
— — — — — — — the draw strings of the waft — — —
— —
— —
— —
— — — — — — — —· — caked dust — — — — — — —
— —

I have not been able to rid (read this word with an accent) myself of words. But the words, the rain of words, the weather being what it was, with not one day, one hour willing to stand up alone without its weather, the low warm puddles, the reflective mist; these combined to achieve the final opalescence of my presence.

The mist. The size distribution, median and modal size of the drops vary greatly from case to case, according to the method of formation, history of the mist, its age, the wind, temperature and radiation conditions, thickening or thinning tendencies, admixture of smoke or other "foreign" microphytic agents, effect of rain or snow falling into it from under or above.

It is noteworthy that the routine observation of mist as a meteorological element has been confined in all weather services and observatories, to recording the observer's opinion as to whether or not true mist exists at or in sight of his station in life at the time of observation, and 2) the observer's estimate of the degree to which his vision has been displaced or replaced by that of the mist.

— <u>The Encyclopedia Britannica</u>

I, no i, (me, mine, she, her, us) am B(b)eing occluded. The occurrence of words.

The colloidal fog creamed the wide face of the after-noon. The epic of microphytic life besieged the thin, flexible rectangles. I turned to wipe off my face. Later I disappeared from the picture. A low sound, a tracer, moved lowly along the pavements, everywhere. This was barely enough to generate the critical amount of tension necessary for the maintenance of solidity. The words clung to the pages for dear life.

The blue vase on the table was blown to pieces. The other three shots had hit their target and Michel, lying on the floor, in almost the same attitude as he lay at the foot of the fence, stopped moving.
This time he was dead.
— <u>Account Unsettled</u>, Georges Simenon

to be tired of <u>The Bride Stripped Bare by Her Bachelors, Even</u>, Marcel Duchamp

But the Houyhnhnms, who live under the government of reason, are no more proud of the good qualities they possess, than I should be for not wanting a leg or an arm, which no man in his wits would boast of, although he must be miserable without them. I dwell the longer upon this subject from the desire I have to make the society of an English Yahoo by any means not insup-portable, and therefore I here entreat those who have any tincture of this absurd vice, that they will not pre-sume to come in my sight.
— <u>Gulliver's Travels</u>, Jonathan Swift

Mist buckled the page. It snapped to attention while the microphytic alphabet roamed the weather's inversion noting subtle differences. I sat apart. Looking for all the world. My face was paper thin. Murmuring pages. Pressed-pulp rectangular shavings piled razor thin planes through and through the mist and my animation was left suspended.

"I will come," said Peter, but he sat on for a moment. What is this terror? what is this ecstasy? he thought to himself. What is it that fills me with extraordinary excitement?
It is Clarissa, he said.
For there she was.

— <u>Mrs. Dalloway</u>, Virginia Woolf

. . . And were there one day to be here, where there are no days, which is no place, born of the impossible voice the unmakable being, and a gleam of light, still all would be silent and empty and dark, as now, as soon now, when all will be ended, all said, it says, it murmurs.
— <u>Stories</u> <u>and</u> <u>Texts</u> <u>for</u> <u>Nothing</u>, Samuel Beckett

Around him the familiar specters dance their waltz, like moths circling a lampshade and bumping into it, like dust in the sun, like little boats lost at sea, lulling to the sea's rhythm their delicate cargo, the old casks, the dead fish, the rigging and tackle, the buoys, the stale bread, the knives and the men.
— <u>The</u> <u>Erasers</u>, Alain Robbe-Grillet

It was about sixty-five degrees. The mist was crowded. The weather worked through the climate. The manuscript pages were embossed out of the haze as a single indistinct unit. The words rose. They were buoyed up.

Then he tried to see the persons already in the room — for probably at that sociable hour there would be more than one — and among them a dark lady, pale and dark, who would look up quickly, half rise, and hold out a long, thin hand with three rings on it. . . . He thought she would be sitting in a sofa-corner near the fire, with azaleas banked behind her on a table.

"It's more real to me here than if I went up," he suddenly heard himself say; and the fear lest that last shadow of reality should lose its edge kept him rooted in his seat as the minutes succeeded each other.

He sat for a long time on the bench in the thickening dusk, his eyes never turning from the balcony. At length a light shone through the windows, and a moment later a man-servant came out on the balcony, drew up the awnings, and closed the shutters.

At that, as if it had been the signal he waited for, Newland Archer got up slowly and walked back to his hotel.

— The Age of Innocence, Edith Wharton

I turned the page period.

It was a wintry page. Its white body lay wide open. A few miles away a weathercock which had been brought to a standstill scratched the atmosphere. A light rain came through the jellied senses. The page was pocked by my sight.

He did not open it now, but one thought passed through his mind: "Can her convictions not be mine now? Her feelings, her aspirations at least. . . ."

She too had been greatly agitated that day, and at night she was taken ill again. But she was so happy — and so unexpectedly happy — that she was almost frightened of her happiness. Seven years, only seven years! At the beginning of their happiness at some moments they were both ready to look on those seven years as though they were seven days. He did not know that the new life would not be given him for nothing, that he would have to pay dearly for it, that it would cost him great striving, great suffering.

But that is the beginning of a new story — the story of the gradual renewal of a man, the story of his gradual regeneration, of his passing from one world into another, of his initiation into a new unknown life. That might be the subject of a new story, but our present story is ended.

— Crime and Punishment, Fyodor Dostoevsky

Every one in a family living having come to be dead ones some are remembering something of some such thing. Some being living not having come to be dead ones can be ones being in a family living. Some being living and having come to be old ones can come then to be dead ones. Some being living and being in a family living and coming then to be old ones can come then to be dead ones. Any one can be certain that some can remember such a thing. Any family living can be one being existing and some can remember something of some such thing.

— The Making of Americans, Gertrude Stein

It was a misty evening. The weather was not fair. The temperature had dropped. The snowstorm was still only an ice-pack. I had words with the weather.

For Kaoru the suspense had been torturing, and the complete failure of the boy's mission was a heavy disappointment. He did not know what to think. The story that she had become a nun and shut herself off entirely from the world, he was not so simple as to believe. If she was indeed living at Ono, no doubt some lover had secretly installed her there and was looking her up from time to time, just as he himself, all too infrequently, had visited her at Uji.
— The Tale of Genji, Lady Murasaki

All these questions, which refer us to a pure and not an accessory reflection, can find their reply only on the ethical plane. We shall devote them to a future work.
— Being and Nothingness, Sartre

. . . The shredded ray of a streetlamp brought out a bright green section of wet boxhedge. I could also distinguish the glint of a special puddle (the one Krug had somehow perceived through the layer of his own life), an oblong puddle invariably acquiring the same form after every shower because of the constant spatulate shape of a depression in the ground. Possibly, something of the kind may be said to occur in regard to the imprint we leave in the intimate texture of space. Twang. A good night for mothing.
— Bend Sinister, Vladimir Nabokov

I sniffed the page. Halfway down the page, I had stumbled over a cliff; a forgotten word stopped me in my tracks. I felt as if .... AS IF .... as if .... as though .... like ....

~~The mist sniffed about the page. It pulsed everywhere.~~

The weather-bound reader came across the story word for word. This ability which edged through the grey, grey and taupe mist and digested the story could never be that of the wood-titmouse (the gold-crest), the woodshrike (the woodchat), the wood tortoise (sculptured tortoise) or the wood robin (wood thrush). All these ligneous things of slyvan places (a group to which the woodspite [green woodpecker] and the wood star [hummingbird, Calothorax] would also belong) would probably chew up the microphytic print in a much less delicate way.

"Yes, Jo, I think your harvest will be a good one," began Mrs. March, frightening away a big black cricket that was staring Teddy out of countenance.

"Not half so good as yours, Mother. Here it is, and we never can thank you enough for the patient sowing and reaping you have done," cried Jo with the loving impetuosity which she could never outgrow.

"I hope there will be more wheat and fewer tares every year," said Amy softly.

"A large sheaf, but I know there's room in your heart for it, Marmee dear," added Meg's tender voice.

Touched to the heart, Mrs. March could only stretch out her arms, as if to gather children and grandchildren to herself and say, with face and voice full of motherly love, gratitude and humility:

"Oh my girls, however long you may live, I never can wish you a greater happiness than this!"

— Little Women, Louisa May Alcott

If the others had their way, they would nibble and chew the pages, regardless of the words, and make them disappear in order to fatten themselves. Only later would they squeeze them off from behind and letter the soil and grass of the slyvan places below them.

If it were always clear the weather would not be the absorbing subject that it is. No, it is not quite an open book. Out in the open air it is certainly not a closed subject. Now it was giving thought to the season. Weather permitted the words to be sighted.

Who knows? He is gone, inscrutable at heart, and the poor girl is leading a sort of soundless, inert life in Stein's house. Stein has aged greatly of late. He feels it himself, and says often that he is "preparing to leave all this; preparing to leave . . ." while he waves his hand sadly at his butterflies.

— Lord Jim, Joseph Conrad

It was falling on every part of the dark central plain, on the treeless hills, falling softly upon the Bog of Allen and, farther westward, softly falling into the dark mutinous Shannon waves. It was falling, too, upon every part of the lonely churchyard on the hill where Michael Furey lay buried. It lay thickly drifted on the crooked crosses and headstones, on the spears of the little gate, on the barren thorns. His soul swooned slowly as he heard the snow falling faintly through the universe and faintly falling like the descent of their last end, upon all the living and the dead.

—The Dubliners, James Joyce

Despite the fact that the author had scoured this page and the next for some time, the microphytic agent still remained. The author, noting the impossibility of such a task, went on to explain in a footnote the reason for the ease with which our bodies absorbed those of these foreign colonies.

It was in fact due to the fact that each colony secreted a pistol spray of cobalt blue violet bile which, though indiscernible, had been found to aid in the emulsification, digestion and absorption of words. And this particular indiscernible coloring is derived from the decomposition of worn-out red corpuscles, cholesterol, lecithin and inorganic salts.

. . . namely to bring Reason to perfect contentment in regard to that which has always, but without permanent results, occupied her powers and engaged her ardent desire for knowledge.

—Critique of Pure Reason, Kant

Sydney Smith went, in 1798, as a tutor to Edinburgh where he occasionally preached, studied medicine and with Jefferey and others founded (1802) the Edinburgh Review. Moving to London in 1803, Smith lectured with great success upon Moral Philosophy at the Royal Institute and made a host of friends. Moving to Yorkshire, he acted as a magistrate and village doctor. Smith's religion though strong, was of a practical nature. He left his work as a life long lover of justice and truth and his own daughter wrote his memoir.

— The Encyclopedia Britannica

Yeobright . . . left alone creeds and systems of philosophy, finding enough and more than enough to occupy his tongue in the opinions and actions common to all good men. Some believed him, and some believed not . . . But everywhere he was kindly received, for the story of his life had become generally known.

— The Return of the Native, Thomas Hardy

A moist draft turned the page, which seemed to be heavily scented with a human perfume. Another sandwich was picked up. At the first bite a large piece of lettuce came tumbling out. It fell between the tightly buttoned grey cuff and the pale taupe wrist of the holder.

It is enormously true that coincidental with the ability to read is the ability to make copies. Copies have been made of simple, complex sentences, words, microphytic agents and molecules, in the presence of the reader who acts as a catalyst. At the same time, the reader is also continuously re-copying himself.

The next page has millions of things on it. An invisible copy has been made of the following words.

But as the last whelmings intermixingly poured themselves over the sunken head of the Indian at the mainmast, leaving a few inches of the erect spar yet visible, together with long streaming yards of the flag, which calmly undulated, with ironical coincidings, over the destroying billows they touched . . .

Now small fowls flew screaming over the yet yawning gulf; sullen white surf beat against its steep sides; then all collapsed, and the great shroud of the sea rolled on as it rolled five thousand years ago.

—Moby Dick, Herman Melville

The mist licked the edges of the colloidal fog. The book closed and contracted. Two coordinated hands clasped. There was a breathless pause. Any book which ends, should have its end appended to this one.

(ATTEMPT IMPOSSIBILITIES; SQUARE THE CIRCLE; SECRET OF PERPETUAL MOTION; SKIN A FLINT; MAKE A SILK PURSE OUT OF A SOW'S EAR; BRICKS WITHOUT STRAW; HAVE NOTHING TO GO UPON; WEAVE A ROPE OF SAND; PRENDRE LA LUNE AVEC LES DENTS; EXTRACT SUNBEAMS FROM CUCUMBERS; SET THE THAMES ON FIRE; MILK A HE-GOAT INTO A SIEVE; ROMPRE L'ANGOUILLE AU GENOU; BE IN TWO PLACES AT ONCE)

Being occluded
Bounding weather
Lettuce slips into the mist
The heart of an ending
Buoyed up by the beating of falling words
and the palpitations of syntax
Rising words. A word rose
The decalcomania of the jellied senses
copies the reader
as the weather
contracts the book

Once her soiled gloves had been taken care of, Minnie began to settle down. For awhile all was quiet with Mickey there beside her. Then, turning to him with the beginning of a smile on her downy face: "Mickey," she said, "Did you hear that sound? I think we have mice in the house."

— <u>Mickey</u> <u>Mouse</u> <u>Comics</u>

B.

Condensation
The Reader and
the Weather

Perhaps you should read this aloud. Listen. I <u>will jump up just once as you begin to stand.</u> I am holding the book and I am standing. I am making the room for myself. I am stretching. The eyes open and shut. I walk over, I walk over to the window. The world has waited for me to write its name. The air agrees with me. You are no longer reading this book. I am not only reading this book, I am calling someone; I am walking to the kitchen; you need the bathroom.

The paragraph which you are about to read has never been written. You are writing it now. I will write you. I will telephone you. I will ring your doorbell. I am not finished with you. I will answer for you.

If you feel you have nothing to say, pick up this book and say anything from it. Rearrange the words any way you like. The last page is the key. Also, for New Year, I have had you say Happy New Year. In the morning, the word rain brings you Good morning, or Is breakfast ready.

I feel I am ready to talk now. You are talking. I cannot prove that I (you) am reading. Is there enough space for you?

A list of some of the words (temporary definitions) not included

1. agglutinate: to unite or cause to adhere, as with glue or other viscous substance; to unite by causing an adhesion of substances; to unite by cause.

2. capsize: to upset; to overturn as a boat.

3. discursive: 1. moving about from one topic to another: skimming over many apparently unconnected subjects. 2. in philosophy, going from the premises to the conclusion in a series of logical steps, distinguished from intuition.

4. Eohippus: the extinct prehistoric ancestor of the modern horse: they were of small size, had on the forefeet four toes with a rudimentary thumb, and on the hind one three toes, and were found in the lower Eocene of New Mexico.

5. empty: 1. containing nothing; evacuated, void of contents. 2. having no one in it; unoccupied.

6. flame: a stream of vapor or gas undergoing combustion and giving forth light of various colors.

7. hermaphrodite: a bisexual being; a being in which the characteristics are either really or apparently combined.

8. hyperbola: a curve formed by the section of a cone cut by a plane that makes a greater angle with the base than the side of the cone makes.

9. hypostatize: to make into or consider as a distinct substance; to contribute substantial or personal existence to.

10. intercourse: the sexual joining of two individuals.

11. metal: any class of chemical elements as iron, gold, aluminum, etc., generally characterized by ductility malleability, luster and conductivity of heat and electricity: these elements form bases with the hydroxyl acid to form a salt.

12. photoelectric: of or having to do with the electric effect produced by light, especially as in the emissions of electrons by certain substances when subjected to light or radiation of suitable wave length.

13. sorbefacient: producing absorption.

14. sordes: the dark brown matter that gathers on the tongue and teeth in low fevers, consisting of epithelial tissue and microorganisms.

15. suicide: the act of killing oneself intentionally.

16. reify: to treat (abstraction) as substantially existing or as a concrete material object.

17. vivid: full of life; vigorous; lively.

18. wave: 1. a curving ridge or swell moving along the surface of a liquid, running in more or less a straight line at a right angle to the movement. 3. an undulation or a series of undulations in or on a surface. 7. in physics (the word) any series of advancing impulses set up by a vibration, pulsation, or a disturbance in air or as in the transmission of heat, light (photon waves), sound.

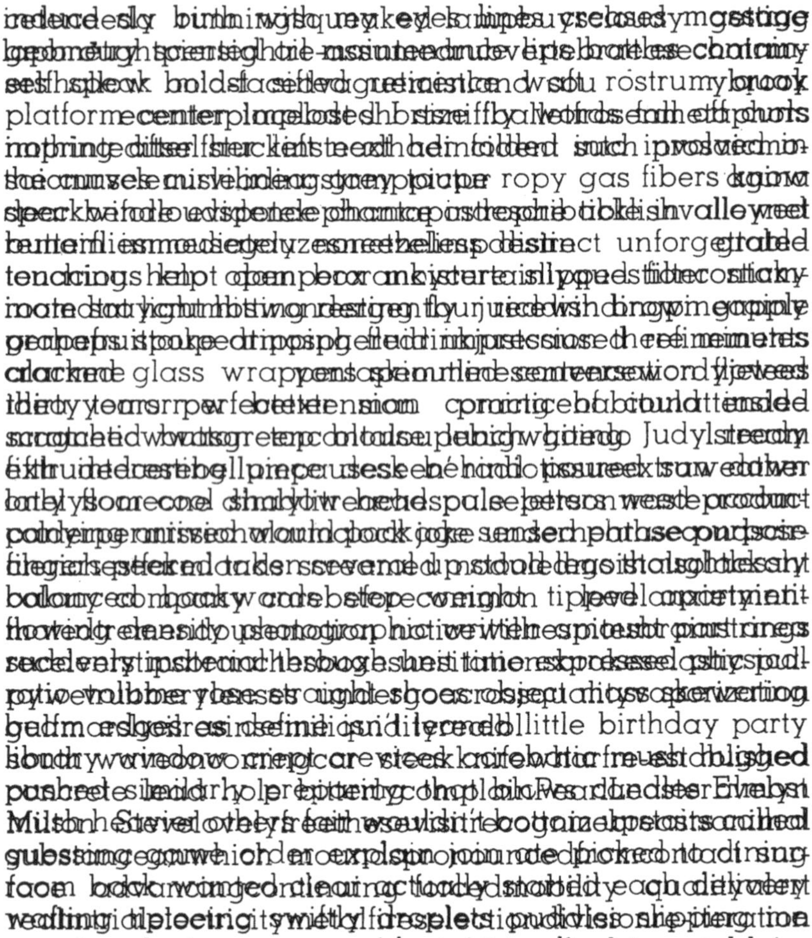

The body is composed 98% of water.

This page contains every word in the book.

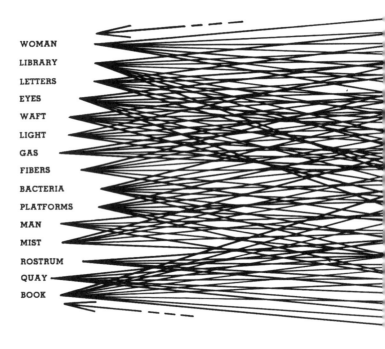

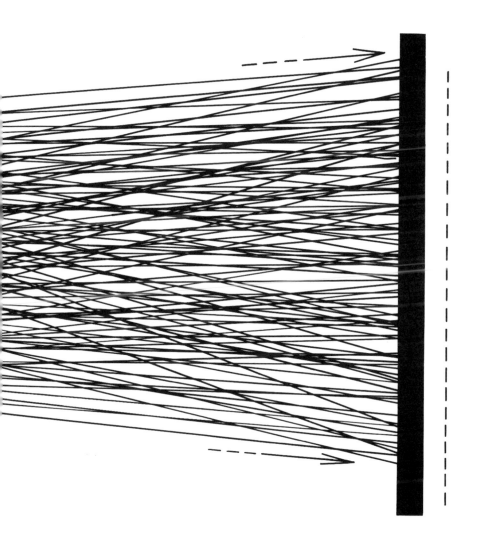

What the President Will Say and Do!!
A Selection

WHAT THE PRESIDENT
WILL SAY AND DO!!

MADELINE GINS

Preface

An early tentative for a planned economy (first begun in o1966), the present work contains ideas / movements of such presidential quality* that undoubtedly (except when it is appropriate to doubt) each of these will sooner or later be enacted.

In which case, this work may be rightly judged to be as predictive as it is prescriptive.

Nobody doesn't want a president who is not a shaman. Similarly, who but a president will ever take epistemology or ontology or even the ravaged Nothing aggressively enough in hand. At such a moment, it could make a big difference who the one in authority is—who is in the position—as they say—to rake through the clicks. We want it to be the President who is the one to pitifully-triumphantly actually pull Nature by the tail.

Not all the alternatives listed here are good, good and Good. No president would read them if they were. Even so, to keep some polish on ethics in general, as a move to upgrade, we do resort to substitutions such as the use of cotton in a stand-in capacity (when in the vicinity of oceans) for a whole host of others, including host, itself, strontium, silk, re-birth (see ahead).

The poem, a practiced president would know that even more than the retrieved configuration in the sense of Mallarmé, and more recently Octavio Paz, it serves best as a stance, one one way or another, a gladiatorial one(!!).

Still, how can we expect those with no practice whatsoever to so configurate themselves. The Poet as the World. Most of the following documents are meant to rectify this situation and . . . . :

---

* crisply embodied tentativity—its apotheosis; the projected in-between; the president as the projector of the visions of others, the puppet head, acquires this quality unique to him by, at all times, saying and doing correctly what has been prescribed.

What the President Will Say and Do!!

FILL THE OCEAN WITH COTTON!

ALWAYS PLACE INFINITE SYSTEMS FACE DOWN.

ALWAYS PLACE INFINITE SYSTEMS.

HANG SIX SCARLET BANDS TO COME WITHIN INCHES OF THE FLOOR.

EVERY CITIZEN SHOULD BE GIVEN A SMALL YELLOW STEAM ENGINE!

KEEP LARGE QUANTITIES OF BRACKISH WATER AWAY FROM EARS.

USE COMPASS TO BISECT EVERY SPOKEN WORD.

ISOLATE BLUE POINTS AND LINES.

MAKE TIME OUT OF WAX.

ENTER A STAIRCASE.

THERE IS NO REASON FOR THIS TO BE WHERE IT IS.

HAVE ALL BIRDS WEAR VEILS TO LOOK MORE MYSTERIOUS!

USE MARBLES (BLUE) INSIDE LONGEST COLUMNS OF GLUE.

ANY CONGRESS MUST WORK ON THE PRINCIPLE OF THE
ARCHIMEDES SCREW.

LOWER THE BIRTH AGE.

I SAID, "LOWER THE BIRTH AGE"

FIRST POUR ALL LEAD INTO THE PAST.

REMOVE ALL INITIAL LETTERS.

SOME PAPER SHOULD BE COMPOSED OF INCIPIENT
EARACHES.

TO BE SURE PASS A WHALE BONE THROUGH A YARD OF
UPENDED GRISTLE.

NOT ALL SENTENCES SHOULD HAVE SAUCES.

ALWAYS CARRY THREE DIFFERENT SCREWS, A HALF
DOZEN NAILS.

(I have nothing to keep them in, *President*)

WHATEVER IS AFFIRMED (DENIED) OF AN ENTIRE
CLASS OR KIND, MAY BE AFFIRMED (DENIED) OF ANY
PART (DICTUM DE OMNI ET NULLO).

PLACE AN EXTRA STRING ON TOP OF EVERY STRING.

"SKIP A FEW DAYS TO LOOSEN THE FLOW OF HISTORY."

USE BOTH ORAL AND RECTAL SENSIBILITY CONES.

POUR ONLY ALONG THE RIGHT SIDE OF ANY CONTAINER!

DIAGONALS SHOULD BE ASSOCIATED WITH SMOKE.

IS THIS QUESTION THIS SENTENCE?

UNCLENCH ROCKS.

USE INVERTED OSMOTIC ENVELOPES.

DO NOT OVER-EMPHASIZE PULSATION IN CITIZENRY.

TURN NOW TO FACE THE WINDOW SAYING: "THERE."

(What should I be doing with my hands at this moment? *R.M. Nixon*)

SUFFUSE MILK WITH THE MEANING OF DOUBT.

TURN ALL BLEMISHES INTO MICRODOTS OF POLITICAL
TREATISES!!

FORBID ATOMS TO LIQUIDS.

EVERY BUILDING SHOULD HAVE A DISTINGUISHED-LOOKING SCAR.

PAINT THREE WALLS MEAD-SYNC AND REMOVE THE FIRST WALL.

KEEP NUMBERS AND STEAM FORCIBLY APART.

"WHEN WILL I NEXT USE: WHEN?"

USE MICE AS DICE.

VERTEBRA TO OPERATE AS ESCALATORS!

MOVE TWELVE FRAYED SPOTS THROUGH THREE DAMPNESSES.

MARK EVERY NON-OBSTRUCTIVE OBJECT WITH AN X.

NURSE CORD.

IMPORTANT: GRAY OBJECTS MAY SUBSUME WIDE ANGLES.

YAWN ONLY INTO SHADOWS.

> (How far is this yawn from my mouth now? *R. Reagan*)

COVER THE INSIDE OF COVERS WITH FELT MUCOUS!

NOTHING *MUST* BE TWISTED.

TAKE ONLY THOSE.

KEEP A SUBSTANTIAL AMOUNT OF CORK NEAR ANYTHING MADE OF PLASTIC.

YELLOW SHOULD ALWAYS FOLLOW BLUE.

KEEP ROWBOAT BEHIND EAR.

ALL SPORTS SHOULD HIRE MICROCOSMS!

WEAR A COPPER PLATE (WITH FOUR HOLES IN IT) ON SOFT PALATE.

SCRATCH HEAD.

MAKE BOTTLE STOPPERS OUT OF HAIRS OF LAUGHTER TWISTED THROUGH WHAT IS LIGHT.

PUT AN ALLOY OF SILVER AND LEAD TIPS ON THE LAST LETTER OF THE LAST WORD OF ALL LAWS.

KEEP *ALL* AIR IN BOXES!

HOLD YOUR NOSE WHEN YOU SEE SOMEONE ELSE'S— INVOLVE MARS.

FAKE WALKING!

BUY USED ACCIDENTS.

USE VISES FOR ATMOSPHERES!

WHEN CLIMBING, EMIT GAS LADDERS.

ON GUARD FOR FALSE LANDSCAPES PROJECTED BY SUN THROUGH GIANT EKTACHROMES WITHOUT EDGE NUMBERS.

MOVING ALL THE WAY UNDER THEN THROUGH (SEVERAL TIMES) THERE APPEARS A VACUUM TUBE WHOSE CRACKED GLASS YELLOWS FROM ASSOCIATION WITH THE AGGRESSIVE DETERIORATION OF THE FILAMENT.

HAIR *WILL* THINK WHEN REINFORCED!

TRY NOT TO UNDERSTAND THIS: MENTION.

ORDER EVERYTHING TO TAKE OUT!

COLLECT BOTTOMS NON-DISCRIMINATORILY.

IF I HAVE THE FEELING OF WHAT DIFFERENCE DOES IT MAKE, WHAT DIFFERENCE DOES IT MAKE?

FOCUS ONLY ON VERTICAL OF ALMOST LIQUID THREE FEET AWAY.

ALL FORWARD MOTIONS SHOULD HAVE THE AROMA OF BURNT ORANGE.

ALL SERVICEMEN MUST HAVE INFINITELY BLUE EYES AND WEAR TWO-HOLED BROWN BUTTONS AT THEIR VANISHING POINTS.

ALL METAPHORS MUST WEAR INTRICATELY OLD-FASHIONED PETTICOATS.

ON THE OTHER HAND, KNOTS SHOULD BE KNEADED
INTO FOAM.(?)

MAKE SALIVA STRINGS INTO COILS.

STAND ON THE RIGHT SIDE OF THE WINDOW FACING
SOUTH WITH HEAD TURNED AT 10 DEGREE ANGLE TOWARD
LEFT OF THE ROOM WHILE REVERTING EYES BACK TO THE
RIGHT SIDE OF THE ROOM AT AN ANGLE OF ROUGHLY 8
DEGREES TO THE MIDLINE.

(Like this? *The Next President*)

TRISECT ONLY IN THE VICINITY OF RESILIENT DILEMMAS.

HERE'S SOME SENTENCE RUFFAGE.

DON'T TAKE THE TOP OFF BUT TAKE THE TOP OFF A CAN OF
NON-VIOLET PRESSURE!

STEER MARROWS!

LAY FARENHEIT SCALE JUST *BESIDE* THE NEXUS ABOVE THE RIGHT EAR.

"WHAT SHOULD I BE DOING WITH MY HANDS?"

LOCATE LATERAL IMPLOSIONS WHICH MAY DESIRE TO PRODUCE CLOUDING.

WEAR SWAMP ARMBAND!

MOVE ALL PRESSURES FROM SIDE TO SIDE ONCE A DAY.

WEAR A RECTUM BUTTON.

"WHO HAS MADE THIS CHAIN OUT OF SCALES FOR WEIGHING?"

IF IT FACES FORWARDS, IT'S NOT IT.

BE SURE YOUR WIFE TAKES HER TUBERCULIN TEST NEXT WEDNESDAY.

(In the morning. *Someone*)

STEP UP THE NUMBER OF REVOLUTIONS PER THOUGHT.

(Per thought. *Someone*)

ASSURE THE TRANSPORTATION OF DAMP MATTRESSES.

ALL RIMS MUST BE SPRAYED WITH ANESTHETIC.

BE GOOD TO EACH OTHER.

STITCH DROPS!

WEAR A SMALL VACUUM CLEANER ON EITHER SIDE OF THE HEAD.

SOME INDENTATIONS SHOULD BE ALLOWED TO RIPEN.

WHAT ABOUT THIS SENTENCE?

.

ONLY DESIRE SPINNING PRODUCTS.

DESTROY ANY ONE NUMBER.

THERE SHOULD ALWAYS BE MANY ENDS OF STRING AT THE DEAFENING CENTER.

ALL POINTS WILL RISE, DRAW CLOSER TOGETHER AT THE
MIDDLE OF MOST MONTHS!

BLEACH WHATEVER IS NOT SEEN TWO OR THREE SHADES.

LIFT ALL CIRCUMFERENCES!

TWO TRANSFORMERS MAY SEIZE OR DESIGNATE A ZONE!

POWDER CURTAINS!

MOVE IT EITHER WAY.

USE SNAKES AS BRICKS AND IRIDESCE!

REQUIRE SHOULDER BLADE PERMITS.

MAKE PARACHUTES THE BASIS OF ALL DREAMS!

ELECTROSTATIC CHEWING GUM.

TAKE ONLY THREE OF THOSE.

ROLL ALL THE CELLOPHANE INTO CRUMPLED BALLS, DROPPING ONLY ONE OR TWO. REACH DOWN AND PICK UP ANY LIQUID FOUND ON AMBER OR AMBER-COLORED PLASTIC. WHERE ARE THE RUBBER TIPS TO MINIMIZE STATIC ELECTRICITY? NOW, TURNING HALFWAY AROUND, DISREGARD ALL IN SEARCH OF POSSIBLY CORROSIVE SPECKS (8 OR 9?), AS WELL AS PATTERN OF THEIR ARRANGEMENT.

(What size specks? *Indira Gandhi*)

ONGOING CARTOONS ON EVERY PLANET!

THE SOUTH SHOULD BE MADE OF PAPER.

ACT WITH FORETHOUGHT WHEN USING ANY WORD FOR
THOUGHT BUT THOUGHT.

PREVENT A CONGESTION OF TRIANGLES.

IDENTIFY A LARGE SECTION OF THE COUNTRY WITH
2500 A.D.

> (May I use B.C.? *R. Reagan* No, not there.)

TWINKLE SKULL!

ALL WEARERS SHOULD BE AFRAID OF THEIR JACKETS
WHICH PUSH!

MAKE AN EXCEPTION: CONSIDER ALL CHILDREN FISH.

LOOK EXACTLY INTO THE NORTH-SOUTH.

USE *EVERY* BLOWTORCH!

REPLACE FINGERNAILS WITH LONG TAPERED MAGNIFYING
LENSES.

SET FOUR HORSESHOES INTO THREE CAREFULLY PRE-
PARED (MOUNTED) SLOPES. THESE ARE TO BE JOINED
WHEN ANY CHOPPED SUBSTANCE BECOMES APPARENT
OR AT THE MOMENT INERTIA DROPS TO .3 DEGREES ON
TEMPERATURE LIP. INSIST ON VARIATION, THEN *FULL*
ERASURE.

THE MEMO YOU ARE LOOKING FOR IS UNDER THE PIECE OF
LINED YELLOW PAPER BY THE SOFA.

(Under my foot? *Mitterand*)

NEVER MOVE ANYTHING ENOUGH!

CLAY PIPES MAY BE REQUIRED TO RE-CONNECT ALL VACUUMS.

HAVE BIRDS WEAR VEILS TO LOOK LESS MYSTERIOUS!

TRANSFORM RUBBING ALCOHOL INTO RADIO WAVES!

TAKE THIS SENTENCE OUT!

SMILE IN A COMPLETE CIRCLE WHEN REMOVING EYELIDS OF ANY MOMENT.

MOVE FINGERS *ALWAYS* FROM LEFT TO RIGHT.

SLEEP WITH ONE FOOT IN TWELVE FEET OF WATER.

USE SANDPAPER SLING FOR CHIN.

ALL BEDCLOTHES SHOULD BE FAR AWAY.

ALL SIGNS SHOULD BE DOUBLE: ONE IN, THE OTHER OUT OF FOCUS.

RE-ARRANGE DOGS TO WORK AS MICROPHONES.

SOME SENTENCES SHOULD BEHAVE LIKE ROCKS.

COME BACK.

URGE LANDSLIDES TO SUSPEND THEMSELVES.

MORE IMPORTANT: GRAY ANGLES MAY SUBSUME WIDE
ANGLES WHICH WEEP.

USE FIRE AS A PULLEY.

SOME DRILLS WILL RESPOND TO COLOR.

KEEP ALL BOTTLES COMPLETELY FULL OF CURVES!

TWO MEN SHOULD WALK PAST HERE.

SOME PART OF ALL WATER SHOULD *BEHAVE* LIKE
CARAMEL.

KEEP POUCH OF PHOSPHOROUS INSIDE FALSE UMBRELLA.

COOL INTO STRANDS.

WITH A MICROSCOPIC CONTACT LENS IN ONE EYE, A TELE-SCOPIC ONE IN THE OTHER, FIND NEAREST INSECT WING, ESTIMATE AMOUNT OF MOISTURE PRESENT.

TRY VERTICAL ICE SKATING.

WEAR A MUZZLE IN THREE DIFFERENT PLACES AT ONCE.

"A SWARM OF FLESH-COLORED MOSQUITOES ARE IMPER-SONATING THE DIRECTOR OF THE F.B.I."

FOLD FINGERS. FINGER FOLDS.

KEEP A WOODEN DUCK IN THE CENTER OF ALL MOVEMENTS.

INSTALL / FORBID METALLIC PLASMA.

GO DOWN TO THE STORE BUT DON'T GO DOWN TO THE STORE THEN GO DOWN TO THE STORE.

FILL ALL COTTON WITH OCEAN!

ANY ICE PENCIL WILL DO.

ERECT CAVERNS OF THREE-QUARTER VIEW ELEGANCE.

FILL ALL CUCUMBERS WITH BLOOD.

RESERVE ONE NASAL PASSAGE FOR COUNTLESS SIGHS.

(From where to where? *John Adams*)

GATHER YE ROSEBUDS WHILE YE MAY!

CONSERVE PERCEPTION. STOCKPILE VISUAL PURPLE!

HOMOGENIZE THIS WORD: PUT.

EMERGENCIES SHOULD NEVER BE ALLOWED TO BECOME SUBCUTANEOUS.

DO NOT HAVE BACK TURNED TO WALL WHEN STRIKING MATCHES.

NO PROTOPLASMIC BUBBLES, PLEASE!

PUT PAPER WRAPPERS ON PERCEPTIONS FROM GREAT
DISTANCES.

SIT IN THE BACK OF THE CAR NEAR THE DOOR WITH THE
OPEN WINDOW (JUST A FRACTION). PLAY WITH SOMETHING
ON THE DOOR SAYING:

(It's cold. I'm closing it. *Someone*)

QUADRUPLE EVERY SPOKEN WORD.

ALL GUNS MUST BE BOOMER-RANGS!!!!!

THE REGENERATIVE POWER OF SCOTCH TAPE IN
CONJUNCTION WITH MERCURY SHOULD BE LABELED!

DO NOT ALLOW ANY FIVE MONTHS TO COME TOGETHER.

INSIST ON THE TWO-DIMENSIONALITY OF THE SKY.

DEEPEN LEGS!!

LENGTHEN THE RUNWAYS ON AIRCRAFT CAVIARS.

SLICE ALL DOORS AND JOIN.

ON INSIDE OF LOWER LIP, INSCRIBE FULL NAME.

PUT AN EYE-DROPPER FULL OF GREASE IN EVERY OTHER HOLE.

PUT FLOORS THROUGH PACES.

CONSIDER MOST SOMERSAULTS AFRICA.

PLACE A VAGINA IN HYPOTHALAMUS (if possible).

NEVER USE WATER ITSELF, ONLY ITS TWIN.

USE ONLY SYNTHETIC SLEEP.

URINATE RUBBER! (SAVE BONDS)

PRESS ELEVATORS INTO CLAY!

DO NOT OVERLOOK ANY CUP AS A MONUMENT.

WHEN RUBBING HUGE QUANTITIES OF BUBBLES INTO EYES,
ALLOW NO MORE THAN TWO TO ENTER OPTIC NERVE.

TURN THIS WORD INTO JUPITER: ANAGRAM.

TRY NEVER TO BUILD WHAT HAS NOT BEEN BUILT THE WAY YOU WANT TO BUILD IT!

THEN STORE SURPLUS PERSONALITIES IN CHEESE.

SHORTEN DISTANCE TO INDEX FINGER.

USE ONLY DORSAL SIDE OF ELECTRICITY WHICH NEEDS CHLORINE.

PUT TREMENDOUS EFFORT INTO THESE WORDS: TREMENDOUS EFFORT.

THIS SENTENCE FEELS SO LIGHT ....

(So what? *Someone*)

ALL CHURCHES SHOULD BE HOLOGRAPHS!!

PUT LIVER IN ONIONS!

SOME PAIN (MINE) SHOULD BE THOUGHT OF AS JEWELRY.

PASS ANTENNAE THROUGH STRAINERS.

CARBONATE FURTHER HOPE FOR SPREAD.

THERE HAVE BEEN WOODEN DISKS MADE OF GAS JUST
ABOVE THE SINUSES.

MOVE CLOSER TO WIFE-LIKE OBJECTS THROUGH
EXCITEMENT.

NEVER USE A MEASURING ROD LONGER THAN FOUR FEET
TEN INCHES WHEN DEALING WITH EMOTIONS.

CAUSE THIS WORD TO FAINT: ALREADY.

EARPHONES CALL FOR GIANT SPONGES.

SPREAD THE MEASLES METAPHYSICALLY!

SIT IN THE STRAIGHT-BACK CHAIR NEAR THE LAMP, PULL
LEFT PANTS LEG DOWN A LITTLE FURTHER. IT SEEMS TO
BE CAUGHT ON THE SIDE.

SCRAPE BUT DON'T SCRAPE AN AMPLE SECTION OF A
WOODEN DUCT DIVIDED LENGTHWISE.

HELICOPTERS ARE EPISTEMOLOGICAL ENTITIES!

SOME THINGS MUST NOT!

EMPTY *ALL* RECEPTACLES!

WRAP AS MANY STEEL RODS AS POSSIBLE IN WHITE
AND BROWN SILK. PLACE IN HORIZONTAL POSITION, IF
NATURE IS APPARENT, APPLY VALVES AT THAT MOMENT.
USE MORE NUMBERS. IS THE LIME IN THE CLOCK?

DO NOT ALLOW ALL TEXTURES TO BE PLACED IN
PERSPECTIVE.

KEEP ONLY THE BACK OF OBJECTS FACING FORWARDS!

ONE PANE OF EVERY WINDOW IS WRONG!

SWITCH FEET WITH FRIEND!

USING FIVE DEGREES FROM IN FRONT AND 3 DEGREES
FROM THE LEFT NUDGE 4 DEGREES FROM THE PERIMETER
TO BEHAVE.

KEEP PEAS WOUND!

PUSH THIS WORD THROUGH PASSER-BY'S HANDBAG.

UNDULATE MOST ARCHWAYS.

DISAGREE WITH WHATEVER COMES BACK.

"THERE ARE NO BRAKES!"

BUILD A BRIDGE OVER THE PAN AM BUILDING!

POIGNANT MOMENTS ARE A DOLLAR EXTRA!

GO FROM CHAIR TO EUSH!

INTEGRATE WHITE AND SWEET POTATOES!

RAKE THROUGH CLICKS!

ORB!

"TUNNELS MUST CONTAIN TUNNELS!"

ALL ACTIONS AND OUTCOMES FOR ALL CITIZENS TO
BE PROJECTED IN A LIT UP BALL WHICH SITS IN THE
CENTER OF EACH VILLAGE!

"BRAIN SHOULD BE THE NEGATIVE WASHCLOTH FOR THE
SOUL!"

TURN ANYTHING AROUND AND AROUND FOR ONE DAY.

AMOEBAS SHOULD ALL FACE IN THE SAME DIRECTION!!

A SECONDARY USAGE FOR PENIS: PAPERWEIGHT!

DROP WORDS OUT OF CONVERSATION AND SHATTER!

LIFT ALL CIRCUMFERENCES!

READ YOUR OWN LIPS!

SOME CONCLUSIONS TO BEHAVE AS PARACHUTES OR
RIVERS!

The Leader I.

"And I would emit gas ladders." The Leader turned toward a swarm of flesh colored mosquitoes. He handed over the cooled strands of one of his newly acquired spinning products.

He went fishing last week. That morning had been spent in making time out of wax and incidentally shaking all waves.

He was sitting in a chair with a straight back. He pulled one pants leg down a little further with a sharp jerk.

"In this situation, I don't want to use any measuring rod longer than four feet ten inches," he insisted.

Using an ice pencil he wrote out the forbiddance of metallic plasma using inverted osmotic envelopes he thought of smoke as the pencil began to melt toward the diagonal.

When he came to the when, he looked up and said,

"When will I next use "when?""

Though both eyelids of the moment vanished even that didn't seem to be enough. There is no reason for this sentence to be where it is. Numbers were being kept forcibly apart from........

Not only that, all his pressures were being moved...

On the phone again he heard!

"What do you mean nothing *must* be twisted?

And he replied:

"Urge landslides to suspend themselves!"

He thought for a moment, made the appropriate substitution and then continued: Let me "scrape" some more and call you back.

As usual his fingers were moving from left to right. He folded them. One nasal passage became deeply filled with sighs. Once he had wound the little green pea, his legs began to deepen.

In the North-South to which he looked for support, rocks un-clenched. All that was left of the South was paper.

"Lateral implosions desiring clouding" was announced.

There were always many ends of string near the deafening center. Short pieces of string had been ground to mush; that which had previously reinforced the tightening valves, revealed now a startling resemblance to neutral chunks (cross-section view). Twelve frayed spots moved through three dampnesses. Although the doors had been previously sliced, the cucumbers were *still* filling up with blood. (It was now an open question as to whether the drills would respond to color and permit the synthesis of a new sleep.)

"What should I be doing with my hands at this moment?"

His fingers were folding again. "I have nothing to say." Standing on the right side of the window facing south with his head turned at a ten degree angle toward the left side of the room and his eyes reverting back to the right side at an angle of approximately 8 degrees to the midline, there *were no* large quantities of brackish water near his ears.

Walking to the phone he crushed the odor of burnt orange. A pile of cork was toppling over onto the plastic dial plate of the phone. In an effort to straighten up the desk, he opened his fly, took out his penis and placed it as a paperweight on top of the mounting pile of papers.

On the top sheet these words were written each twice once in, once out of focus: insect wing. Just beneath a fly wing was pasted on top of a drawing of how it should look. All these signs were becoming drenched by the chlorine which poured out from the telephone wires. It was running in a stream down the *right* side of the desk. Having neglected to bring his contact lenses with him to the office, he left the saturation study for another time but he did take advantage of the situation by putting a paper wrapper on that perception.

He turned now to face the window: There.

He didn't exactly scrape a section of a wooden duct on the other hand knots were being kneaded into foam and there was a duck in all movements, wooden, that is.

The major thrust of the speech would be the de-emphasizing of pulsation among citizens on every level. There would be the presentation in the name of the state of small yellow steam engines!

Yet awhile before wax had been prevented from becoming time so that despite the hold up blue points and lines were all the more isolated and there was the assurance of the separation between **steam** and . . . . .

Only one bubble was allowed to pass through the optic nerve. The rest of the air was already in boxes. He saw from the window a huge formation of two-hole brown buttons threading past the window. Only one hole of each button was filled with grease. Damp mattresses were whizzing by in government vans. Two men walked by here. He drew an X of knotted foam across the window pane.

Then he walked to the door, asked the gentlemen who had been waiting an unusually long time to come in. He took only three packages from them. He thanked them for making it possible for him to go down to the store but not to go down to the store, then go down to the store. A coil fell from his lips.

Attempting to remove the cover from the milk bottle, his fingers became numb, hairs of laughter had to become untwisted from whatever was light before he could open it. Doubt became suffused with milk to such an extent that finally the liquid seemed not to contain atoms, the bottle filled up with curves completely. He spit into the cover, smoothed the coils. Then he passed around triangles of meat taking care to avoid a congestion of triangles.

As many steel rods as possible were wrapped in white and brown silk, placed in horizontal position. At the throw of mice* he dropped words out of conversation, shattered:

"THE brain should   negative for   "

Later that day, stepping up to the podium, the electrostatic chewing gum rubbed up against his full name inscribed on his lower lip. He stood there with wooden discs of gas above the sinuses, turning around and around, with a small vacuum cleaner on either side of his head.

Now two transformers designated a zone; rubbing alcohol was tuned into radio waves. Raising arm to signal, once in focus, once out, the beginning of his speech, he shortened the distance to his index finger which strove from left to right. He smiled in a complete circle.

He meant to say: "There are no brakes!"

* dice

But instead he said: Fish** must grow up to become each other!

"Do not overlook cups as monuments"

".se   .very   .low-orch"

A task force of helicopters hovered above.

The president took this opportunity to say: Mars while holding his nose and taking some other indeterminate actions.

There were some other phrases without initials and then:

"I said lower please the birth age." He signaled for it to begin.

"Poignant moments are a dollar extra," he cried out.

A man in a blue suit, blue tie was the first to leave. Seconds later a gentleman in a yellow tie (C.I.A?) on the other side of the room ran out after him.

The President yawned into the shadows (now!).

Every once in a while he would look through his finger nails at a freckle, then read off an interesting historical quote. Why had the small yellow steam engines not yet arrived from the factory. It was getting late; he adjusted his swamp armband.

Meanwhile the antennaes were being strained. All birds wore veils to seem more mysterious, then less mysterious. The Leader was not the one to take the top off a can of non-violet pressure, though he did stay late; he

** As children

was still there after everyone left, putting an extra string on every string left uncovered. Many of these were at the deafening center.

On the way home, he stopped at the office to put an alloy of silver and lead tips on the last letter of a statement just signed into law that waxed morning: Fill the ocean with cotton!

As soon as he reached home, he reminded his wife about her tuberculin test next Wednesday. He waved to his children in the pond. He rubbed some balm into the kheloid scar on the back porch.

His bedclothes were still faraway. There were no wide angles in front of him, only gray objects.

Thinking of saving bonds, he was pleased to find himself urinating rubber. He un-buttoned the button, removed the sensibility cone. His sister caught the measles because of him, although she was faraway on paper.

Moving closer to the wife-like object he became more excited. He did nurse cord. Only the shadow of a vagina [was placed] in his hypothalmus. The farenheit scale lay just above the nexus of the right ear in front of the rowboat. The left side was sweet, the right sour.

Then the wife-like object placed a pile of papers near her anesthetized Southern rim. He set himself upon these. Using this as an outsized compress, he was still unsure whether to nudge potential energy into either finity or infinity.

Alas, it was only next door that the marrows were being steered while a whalebone passed through a yard of upended gristle. It was *across the street* too that a staircase was entered. This is the first time this sentence is being used and some sentences should not have sauces. (sources?)

Alas the receptacles were emptied, the emergency was not allowed to become subcutaneous. As twelve frayed spots moved through three dampnesses he became anesthetized by the rim, took off his jewelry.

Taking the numb paperweight in hand, he made sure to turn it around and around. To his wife he said:

"After all honey, all metaphors should wear intricately old-fashioned petticoats......I (as he yawned into the shadows) think it will be from tomorrow on that I will skip a few days just to loosen the flow of history....you see, in that way, we might be able....or....(and just before his final evening somersault, he was heard to say:) Look around, look around, have I or have I not—I can't remember—(and just as the lateral implosions were producing the desired clouding:) Have I secured a lower birth age?"

(Fade, fade out.........)

The Leader II.

Still hands were kneading knots into foam.

Once "Important: Gray object may subsume wide angles" had been read, the administration earnestly set to work to restore the White House and the horizon. No one considered that this might be just a hangover (tongue in cheek) from a period which had for a short while been dominated by minimal art. Furthermore, already they had begun to paint three walls mead-sync and to remove the first wall.

Smoke and diagonals were freely associating. The restorers would even go so far as to powder the curtains, if necessary.

He or she sat in the straight back chair rather near a lamp. He or she had some trouble pulling down the left leg-sleeve of his/her trousers—it having become caught on . . . was it a nail or a certain rough spot in the leg of the chair itself? No one in or out of the world of fiction could be sure. Inevitably he-she thought of scraping but not scraping an ample section of a wooden duct divided lengthwise. Wasn't it, after all, he or she who had promised to peg all traces. Well, that infinite system had been finally placed downwards (falling) for awhile.

This was heard (the voice:male or female): "I (cyclone to cyclone) would without a doubt (this doubt happened to be milkless) continue to emit gas ladders!"

Then a variety of objects passed hands, including some cooled strands, an extremely desirable spinning product, a substantial quantity of both the tuneful and non-melodic varieties of cork. There is no reason for this sentence to be where it is. Similarly there is no reason for this sentence to be where it is, but if it faces forwards, it's not it.

The President knew:

NUMBERS WERE BEING KEPT FORCIBLY APART FROM . . . . .

. . . .

As on the phone he heard:

"Whadya mean 'nothing *must* be twisted!'?"

The reply came:

"Begin by urging (strongly) landslides to suspend themselves"

. . . . he . . . thought for a moment, making the appropriate substitution . . . . so that she could continue . . . . . with: "Let me 'scrape' some more and call you back."

As usual his or her fingers were moving from left to right. He folded them. She folded them.

A nasal passage which was so extensive that it might be considered a narrow-corridor continuation of the already greatly deepened legs was, at that moment, just full of sighs. But no protoplasmic bubbles, please.

They looked directly into the North-South, this leader, from whence was wafting multi-dimensionally the sound of the unclenching of rocks and of several stations of erstwhile alcohol.

. . . . STEAM.

She and he had so much to say and do to artists, the art world, butchers, physicians, nurses and architects. . . . and so much to say and do to others. All of it prescribed . . . . and more of it . . . . to be . . . . prescribed. Much had been done: Judging Procedure, War Policies, Fire Directives had all been established along more or less poetic lines (see following); yet, much remained to be done: When, for example, would this president begin to say and do things to/through h(im)erself and come truly to inhabit his/ her puppet head.

All Men are Sisters
(including A Sisterly Thesaural Dictionary)

Woman is the host. Man, the guest (guestess?). But the host has been too amiable for too long. Look at what we have bred. We have acquiesced to such a degree that in our own homes we now speak their language instead of ours.

Men are by nature critical. Women, self-critical. This is the critical difference.

There simply could not have been a woman who would have said, "Left side," "right side," then stuck to it. For a woman, it is a question of at least seven sides, at least one for every hue. Such subtlety contributes to the subtle difference.

One thing men haven't realized is that unlike them (all men are mortal), women do not die—*This makes all the difference*—although some women, having been brow-beaten by sheer syllogistic brawn, have at times pretended.

Most women do not look like themselves; although many women do assume the form of "woman," some are men, others gas and electricity, and still others are indistinguishable.

Often, being constructed of living material, women are a volatile force in society and as such dangerous and should be kept away from adolescents (many of these themselves women), as St. Thomas Acquinas was perceptive enough to discover.

But there does not exist enough perception to cover this field.

Bringing in the notion of man (in Japanese: *otoko*) might be helpful. Man gives a notion of what "woman" (*onna*) is like at her worst. A better way to say this is that all that has not been understood by or about "man," that is beyond "man's" reach, is innately "woman." But this is not saying it either. How could it? I am using our communal language which is man's. A woman would never phrase a concept like that, not left on her own.

I use "woman" in several senses.

Women do not enjoy molecular behaviour. They are of a different stature.

Woman's ontological regions are labile. She is a cross-animation, having achieved crossed-references through extenuated tendencies and translatory extra-curricular reflexes. As such, any woman's ontology is doubly immanent and compounded to any man's. Who else could have formed itself from a rib, which remains true whether true or false? When prevailed upon, she performs amazing feats, but these ought not to be viewed as prerequisites for animation. Only those with voices as we have known them up till now would say otherwise. Knowledge is like porridge: without the milk of a generative ontology it remains dry, if not tasteless. That's also how tact gets lost.

If William Blake were not a woman, he was not. Partially, he was. Drawing lambs from combs, listing gorillas into rhomboids, suffusing "willing" with Eurydice. Isles of limps having *wiltern* scents bask in under repose deposits summa. Then peek into the oven to see if it is done. We know (in the winking ridges heading towards our vowels' soup of muscles; dew). Also, it is clear.

"Playing with himself, he became her."

"She said nes."

Over here. The steambath. Do you see it? It is all over.

They have made a culture (tiny) in our culture, but it is all over. Rimbaud knew and so did George Washington. The host is shrugging the world.

If George Washington never was a woman, he . . .

I am not sure which way it is, whether I say what I'm feeling more than I feel what I'm saying or the other way around. Retracing the steps. Is it a series of mutual tuckings? "Woman" lives there.

Women are always in the spotlight (rough translation). That is why it is never dark. Of course, if I were more specific, this would become too light.

The host is more than ambiguous, as well she must be. How else could a glance become a fragrance, a fragrance a warp, a warp a dish, a dish a fountain...pen? Or rather, how too could this be prevented from happening?

A Sisterly Thesaural Dictionary

Notes for a Guidebook
to the Fictional Exercises of the Dictionary

Existence:
    Employer
    Uses Conveyor and Conversion Processes
    Mercurial
    Having Recourse to . . .
    Not for Everyone
    Junta

Inexistence:
    Total Lack of Motivation
    Orange Colored

Substantiality:
    Any Thickness found Through Thinness
       (Breathing)
    Trial Exposure
    Basis for Photography

Unsubstantiality:
    Nothing More Than Seven Syllables Adjoined
    Pour Through Fissures of this Word:
       Toward the Discovery of a *Quadruple*
       Hypnotic Vapour!

Intrinsicality:
    Closest to "Pressure" of Fiction
    Bubbles Which Refer to Straight Lines, Etc.
    Opacity Disguised as Transparency
    A Hit

Extrinsicality: A Fermenting Spray
When Allowed to Harden May be Peeled,
Soaked in an Indifferent Solution and
Applied Intrinsically
Glas

Increase: Spontaneous Repetition of Edges
Spinning Directional Budding
Aggregate Notion:
Take Lower Lip Between Thumb and Forefinger
Pull Out as Far as it Will Go.

Decrease: Often Misunderstood
Multiplication of Chance Partings
A Whip

Addition: Operating on the Skeletal Forces of *Increase*
Roughly Powder Form of Increase
Can be Colorful
Collected Walking

Subduction: Powdered Decrease
Used with Softest Brushes and
A Network of Flews
Feels Backwards

Adjunct: Filling in of Blanks
May be Substantial
The Back of a Flying Sink

Remainder: One Sum of *After's* Qualities
Possibility for Poignancy
For Example, Frogs from Tadpoles

State:
　　Production of Directions
　　William's View
　　What is Connected to this Sentence.
　　Other Insertions

Circumstance:
　　Collection of Angles in Which a Knotted Current
　　　　Is Allowed to Pass Through Making Notches.
　　Anything Which Permits Analogy to Another
　　　　Thing or Process (The Way in Which this
　　　　is Backwards?)
　　Tight Boots
　　Pierced Scrotum

Mean:
　　Probably *Not* Made of Cork Though There is a
　　　　Great Resemblance
　　As if Medium-Sized Fan in Between
　　A Skirted Locus
　　Arrival On

Compensation:
　　Overlapping Fires Ore Reflections of These
　　Re-Filling of Particles
　　Reaction of X to an Unknown Form of Massage

Greatness:
　　Into the Collapsed Measure

Smallness:
　　Toward Which Anything Shrinks
　　Only What is Noticed Approximating the
　　　　Size of Irreducible Points in Receivership
　　Retracted Scratch
　　Blandness or

Superiority and Inferiority:	The Back and Front of Yawning and Dogmatism
	Very Heavy or Much Too Light
Pre-Cursor:	Cloth Dipped in Semen and Re-Hidden Daily in Caves of Space
	A Jet Hook
Sequel:	One Translation of Coded Beats (or Beets!)
	Mildewed Fear
	Final Rinse
Beginning:	Weighted Zero
	Largest Collector
	May Employ Suction Cone
	Super-Imposition of Endings
	A Surprise Symptom
	As Butter or Ice Cream Form . . .
End:	Expansion of Amnesia
	Obsolete
	Massive Brushing Aside in Depth
	One Result of Idiocy
	Unresolved in Spite of Implications
Middle:	Damp or Burning
	Hard or Soft
	Intense and Fuzzy
	Restless

Continuity:

Discontinuity: Partial Vacations In and Out
Perception of Cells as Splinters
A Suppuration of Lightning

Mixture: A Rotorized Marbleization of Increase and/or
Decrease
Always Pretty at Times Volatile

Simpleness: One Symptom

Vinculum: Looped Delight with Shading
The Metal Part of Cheese Which Has Been Forged
A Point (All?) Moving in Two or More Directions at
Once

Rub the Sheerest Vinculums Together Incessantly!

Coherence: Buckling in Conjunction with Stamping
A "Y" Which Almost Exists
Retention or Pretention of Currents in Currents
Evidence of the Ability of the Internal Structure
Of a Push to Relate to Itself
Candy
Amalgam of Seven (Or More) *Temperatures* (And/Or
Fevers?)

Incoherence: Opened (And Held Open) Coherence
The Explosion of a Push
Convoluted Elasticity Which Tends to Prevent
Itself
Evidence of Spotting or Spotty Evidence

Remove Fibers!

Combination: Juggler of Holes
The Locking and Triggering of Numbers on
    Location
For Example: The Use of Iron Swabs in the Easing
    Of Aluminum

Tight Fits

Order: Dial Tone

Disorder: A Gas Slip Causing Wild Redundancies(?)
Product of Thyroid Shivers
Manifested as Lack of Traction: (1) Of the General
    In General (2) The General in Specific (3) The Specific
    In General (4) The Specific in the Specific.
Also, The Accidental Occurence of Secretion
    During Measurement.

Must Be Kept in Working Order!

Arrangement: See Lay-Out Here

Derangement: Same as 'Disorder' But With Slightly More
    Expandable Tone. Perhaps with Own Colors:
    Brown and Scarlet?
Clinging Severs

Precedence: Any Sequel to Origin
A Long Pliant Board
End Point(s) of a Trembling Which is Finished
A Particular Giraffe Which is Known to Appear
    Always Before Another Kind
Evidence: Used Tufts

Sequence:	One View of the Appearance of a Gerry-Mandering
	Employing Synthetic Yeast
	In Association with Sliding but Rigid Fictions
	Thresher of Outlines Into/Through Tunnels
	Organic Only at the Roots!
Decompositions:	Method of Force-Feeding Poor X To Y
	The Technology of Dust
	Self-Aspirating Environments
	Growth Pattern of Mechanical Disaffection
	One of Many Things Which Have Happened to the Past
	Under the Sign of the *Unreliably Predictable*!

How to Breathe

A nose and a mouth on the subject initially. (e.g.), (i.e.), (n.b.). Will that, such a recognition, cause you to hold your breath? If so, then be ready to admit that you have experienced a false start.

Just consider the apparatus as closely as possible and don't give a thought to suicide yet.

Do *not* breathe now. Time enough once everything has been fully explained. At this point, all I ask of you is to not pamper your ego nor to too willingly succumb to the contaminated will engendered by the gay abandon of the societal rot of centuries.

As support for the neutral position I here suggest, I might state that, inexorably, *nothing* (oh yes, absolutely) will come of an abortive attempt in this area.

Remember, too, breathing is no lark (not even nine-and-twenty blackbirds baked in a pie, I would think).

Then let us first take a figurative breath which will entail:
1. Selection (determining "breathability" of gases)
2. Choosing of path of entrance (there is some choice)
3. Determining of length (here, space is again a function of time)
4. a) Generating of anatomical readiness (also, composite)
   b) Bearing appropriate dimensions
5. Sucking
6. Propagation of sucking (and its derivatives) for the sake of transportation.
7. a) Electrical flow
   b) Expansive desire

8. Entering and expanding
9. Spreading
10. Attaching (in each sense)
11. Applying (applies even when indeterminate)
12. Rejecting (there are gradations)
13. Collapsing
14. Inviting of pressure play
15. Expulsing (and to the new breath back to 1)

At the subject once again (if you do not remember...?), what do we notice but a cohesive series of supporting, often participating, structures various in form and function but of common purpose.

There is a box of muscle designed with a slit comfortable enough to be a hole. Tubes grown together (almost appearing to have been taped into place), having hammered through thickets, lead along three or four alternate paths to the 300 million, 1/250th of an inch thick, inflatable containers of below. Here, all along this, and below, one is given room to breathe, here, towards the center of the earth.

Locked into moist tubularity, the would-be tubes have branched so as to reach with the currents with which they will one day be filled to the back, front and sides of the body which will cling to them or appertain.

Palpitating chunks palpating and chunks of palpitations as well as palpitations becoming chunks and slivers ride the nearly snapping membranes which shuffling side by side adduce, as some see it, further layers along that passageway which often bespeaks the notion of: HERE.

[To have gulped . . . . to have haustrated]

Where muscles the thickness of the tongue line sliding walls, notches and folds have learned or come to complement each other.

Here geometry is the secret host to fancy and the other way around, too.

Still we find both a nose and a mouth on the subject. And more can be said about this.

"We never live, but we ever hope to live." *Pascal*

"A good face is the best letter of recommendation." *Queen Elizabeth*

"Sweet spring, full of sweet days and roses, a box where sweets compacted lie." *Herbert*

. . . . How often in the past has the nose been mouthed? And really to what degree can a nose be mouthed and not just merely spoken of? But even more significant is our inability truly to discern how satisfied, in fact, each of these structures is with its own shape. How directly have these cartilaginious or labilely prominent members ever been addressed? As usual the subject has only been sniffed at thus far. Then what is being said to what when "Look what shape you're in!" is expressed [expressed].

The aquilinity and the gash. And that nostrils will spring to such subjects in whose junctures mouths lie? Mother? Money? Memory? Are these fitting [fitted] subjects? Falsehood? Debt? Contradiction? Confession? Honor? Sympathy? To what are these subjected, after all? A subjugation of shapes dominates the impressionism of physiognomy, and what else adheres?

But a few spots below face level, violet and brown strings manage to stay as they are. From birth, these commence to sway unceasingly across layers. The forming of a question, for exit, takes place around and about this sway. Is there anything which is not a question when it is about this sway?

As many cords as necessary, for the time being (that carved parenthesis), are covered with human scales (this part is true). Fitted into the subject's voice box, these sway against a mesh of pipe dreams dreamt or made with flexible precision. So much for dreams which are galvanized. [To galvanize from within...]. Their fine reputation comes from the vast amount [all] of sculpture which they have initially inspired. (Once you breathe, you will see what sculpture is.) Fragile, of ancient origin, these boxes, might it be that there are no originals left... only records...

A thirsty description. But it is suggested that it is here that breath shall be enacted. Reenacted. It is felt that a certain percentage of the atmosphere could wash through going this way.

Don't breathe now.

No, no dream of beginning this yet! How could you? Even a... brilliant practitioner could not yet... but a mere amateur... the heartbeat of an amateur... Please wait [soon to be available (or never?) by the same author: *How to Wait*].

How to ascertain which is it, the cat or the bird, which has got your tongue(?).

It could be that occasionally a complete(d) mouth will smile and open pulling whatever drifts nearby down into its portable tree. Safeguard against this, for the moment. Don't hold your breath (or take in air) until you have mastered this article just hold your non-breath.[1]

Just think what might have happened if hitherto you had attempted a breath without having been told: Oxygen is the sought-after element and carbon dioxide the compound to be expelled.

Hold on!

An 860 square foot surface is to be oxygenated (the path is 1,500 miles long) in less than 1 second.[2] Can you feel you have that in you? Lungs only look useless to you now; consequently, don't discard what may appear for the moment to be only extra tissue baggage.

Any object which happens to stray into the lungs invariably ends up in the right lung; this is because the lungs are assymetrically disposed with the direct path from the mouth going to the base of the right bronchus. There are three lobes on the right side, only two on the left. This may be true in ghosts, as well.

Some arguably poorer species have eyes which double as lungs. Lungs coalesce, at times, into a whole host of oddities.[3]

I know you do not yet feel the need to breathe, but remember, lungs never truly come into their own until they do. Until they do, they remind one more than anything else of foam, of which they are the sophisticated relative. Actually the sophistication comes with use. The organizing principle, once put into play, causes the lungs to operate as cohesive foam which itself participates in the generating of waves.

If you have not betrayed my confidence, you have not breathed yet. And what is breathing?? Whatever it is, let it continue where it may while you, for just a little while longer, continue to keep your distance. You see once you will have started, you had better not stop, ever. And you will make it wide. The time for the first breath draws near. At this point, if there continues to be a lack of interest in you about this, this might be the moment at which suicide could be tried more painlessly than ever again... before we go on, if you like.

Breathed. History was. Breathing will be found to be a prerequisite for:

1. Getting a license
2. Finding a job
3. Having children

4. Starting a revolution
5. Being an idiot
6. Laughing

Anxious? No psychiatrist in the country would touch your case unless he/she were sure (assured?) that you were breathing.

Once you have begun and are breathing, nothing will be the same. You will, however, find yourself gaining weight under this regimen. There will be an accompanying hum which you might find disturbing at first...and a faint, erotic trembling comes with it...one which totally eludes prefiguring (the purest of aporias).

(Let this be a breathless pause)

Think (but not a step further!): your mouth has been opened; some atmosphere, roundabout, naturally, enters. You would do well to concentrate on the perceiving of this atmosphere as much thinner and much more penetrable than you are. You see, a part of breathing, is the wanting of this substance, ethereal as it is, to be inside of you. Work hard at believing this to be desirable.

Try moving your hand across the neighboring air, patting then stroking it. Do feel the mounting of its desirability. When moving about so, why not wave some of this air right into your, after all, visibly open ear. Using the ear for practice, take a would-be breath through it, Dear non-Breathed Sub(ject)stance. For a measured breath, assume a pair of earlips have closed about some set amount of gulpable atmosphere. Or keeping your mouth just as closed as it ever was, wave some air past it, too, while imagining it might be open. Then, quickly, think of wanting air. Slowly beyond slowly, think of wanting air. What a strain for you now, but one day it will be unimaginable not to take this into consideration—either regularly or urgently.

Envision a plane of muscles three inches below your breast line. This is almost yours; think of it as an ally. The movement of the diaphragm—when it comes—will be an up and down one; it will benefit the stomach as well.

Time nears. But wait. Potential gestures of real strings (nerve jute[4]) send wishes. The thumb of one of these taps then prods what ought to have been innate. For it is into the cave of innateness the traveler must go. In there, you will get to be breathed. Over some hommunculus' nose flows what will become the breath through yours. Perhaps the hommunculus is nothing more than the head of a pin or the pip of a chromosome.

And so beginning or relenting is here.

You might breathe now.

Get breath.

You might breathe now.

You might breathe now.

You might breathe now.

And now.

This time cause your fresh breath to hop. Hop!

Now skip a breath.

Jump into the next breath; make that breath jump, too.

Swing the breath around: this is called around the world.

Make it sit.

Walk it.

Take a running breath and leap into _____.

Breathing is just like _____.

Reader: have you breathed? Had you noticed when I let the cat out of the bag? In order to determine the instant when breath first started in you, go back into the text to find the point at which the words (upon which you with your amateur's awkwardness will have inevitably imposed) first appear fogged (??).

(You might breathe now.)

(Breathe) I am technically rather an amateur at this myself. In fact, several people, including myself, feel that I am unqualified to write an article such as this. (But breathe about now.) Yet much of what is written here could be (shall be) highly breathable. I leave it to the experts to explain how to move *through* breathing, I just deal with getting *in* and *out.* The value of such practice cannot be overestimated. Never in, one enters, as today, but once put out, how can one ever get back in? Perhaps one day I will do some work (certainly in collaboration with many others) which will answer that.

Notes

[1] Consult family doctor before taking first breath. Check all x-rays, charts. None of what is said here will apply to you *unless you are made for it.*

If unfit, unfortunately unable to partake of this sport as here described, do not become too soon discouraged. Check the encyclopedia under *Diffusion.* There you may find still another inspiring way to go about this.

If you do appear fit, there is still one more thing I would ask of you—check and double check both your *Genus and Species* before trying anything.

[2] I am referring to a system which works with air. Water vapor hovers about but is not central to the activity. This is in sharp distinction to that old-fashioned process of forcing water up through the gills in direct opposition to the flow of blood, snapping off whole ounces of oxygen to give the organism something to work with; nor is this really analogous to a network of air ducts directly exposed to the environment.

[3] Lungs have been found between legs and dangling naturally from ears. Almost everywhere they are eaten. There have been cases of twelve lungs in one being.

[4] If you ever have anything to do with a nerve, be sure to generate the normal sine curve. Any irregularity would turn up as wheezing or gasping. Death in this case would be a straight line. Move all straight lines.

Whole: A Mouthfull and All Translations of It
What is Put Onto the Scale When Everything Is
Swept Onto It . . . .
A Second's Filling
The Only Distinct Part of Nothing
Completely Absorbent Word (See Above and
Below)

Part: Anything Picked Up (Out) During the Cross-
Sectioning Of a Zone
Any X of a Gesture
Some of Whatever Is Next to a Razor Blade, Cup,
Or Plant.
Anything
In One Case: Liquid With a String Looped Around
It

Completeness: A Translucent Shawl for the Word 'Whole'
May Be Worn in Slightly Different Ways

Incompleteness: Ah!

Composition: Based on Floating Maps
The *Figuring Out*
Master Spy

Term:

Assemblage: Major

Non-Assemblage: From, The To In Or A But Not And

Focus: Partial Evidence of Healing of A Priori Vaccination
Against Blindness
Wave Percolation
A Ball May Be Thrown Into This
Resolution Of Any Of These Words

Class:

Inclusion: As In The Sweep Of Faceted Valves
Generous But Secretive
May Operate Cusps
Open Pairing

Exclusion: True And/Or False Kicking

Generality: Passage Of A Word Through Itself
An Overdose
A Too Fixed "Circumference"

Speciality: Zinc Gambling

Rule: Plant or Plant-Like Formation
A Construction of Sieves: 1) Positive Spaced
2) Negative Spaced
The Separating Out Of Nearly Identical Mysteries
Transplantation Out Of Any (Series Of) Organ(s)

Multiformity: May Be Based on the Eroticism Of The Cardinal
Points!

Conformity: X As Y (Almost)

Uniformity: A Rigid Whirlpool (Pressed) Which Has Become
　　　　　Partially Unfixed
Nude Thoughts
Wind Made of Silver, Etc.

Number: Profiles
Clamps
Also, More Numb

Numeration: The Sum Of The Folds In A Pile Or:
　　　　　It Is Customary To Subtract The Journey
　　　　　Of Currents Through Dust Allowing For Marks
　　　　　In The Distance
A Way Of Accumulating Space Through
　　　　　Tightrope-Walking From One Scale To Another
(One Of These 'Seems' To Be Imperceptible)

List: Record Of The Divisions Of Laughter Or Of
　　　　　What Should Have Been Laughter
Could Be Used As A Multiple Corkscrew
Travelogue
Evidence Of The Production Of A "Meaningful
　　　　　Shell" By A Vertebrate
Make A List Of What Can't Be Said!

Unity: Skip

Accompaniment: "There" With "This"
Taking A Bath
An Oriole To Nerves
As In A Half-Sinking,
　　　　　Half-More Than Floating Tapping

Duality: The Brace Illusion
                The Negative Space Of A Fissure
                Who Is What?
                Re-Fuse Duality!

Duplication: Hopeful

Bisection: This May Really Happen

Triality: Amenable
                Sum Of Every Other Finger On One Hand

Brief Autobiography of a Non-Existent

"chilled reason"
—Three Edgars

This first sentence was very difficult to write. The next sentence should become easier. It is a question of surrounding... Exploring the area between surrounding and entrapment... A lure for motion.

Memory has never been dipped into being born. Without a starting point everything runs by, not nodding. It was about that position that the great poet arranged these words:

> He never was. Never saw, nor felt, nor touch
> tasted. Dreams he had not for he had not life.
> And from that day forward and backwards he never was.

Position

Having nothing to fear or gain, found free to express with nothing to express, it develops that the universe will become bombarded at random with particles that look like "I". These, probability mouths to the dead weight which recounts, these will in all likelihood enter the unrecognizable consciousnesses and establish the distance. I leaned against nothing. The "I", pelted and whirred from beyond any collection of intelligence, started to write. (One of many phrases which "I" picked up.)

I.

1913: I was not born. My mother never existed.

1914: There were no brothers or sisters to play with. I did not live in a large country house with rambling fields about it. Green was completely unknown to me as were grass, trees and the sky out of the question.

1915: A bee did not sting me and cause a high fever which produced strange deliriums from which I still suffer.

1918: I did not begin to masturbate. I had no intention of playing hookey.

1919: My father did not inherit a fortune. My maternal grandmother never died. My unmarried aunt did not come to live with us.

1924: I didn't practice my violin regularly. I never combed my hair. My teacher never noticed me. I did not celebrate my birthday that year because of an illness in the family.

1925: I never participated in sports. No matter what the activity. I was never asked to join in. I never met anyone.

1926: I was not overly protected. I didn't take the Grand Tour of Europe that year. My father didn't bring my frail orphaned cousin into the warmth of our home. I produced nothing of worth yet I wasn't beside myself with worry.

1927: I didn't have an intolerable adolescence. I wasn't self-conscious. We did not move to New York on the occasion of my father's promotion. My father did not quarrel with his immediate superior nor did he rage uncontrollably against my by then bed-ridden mother.

1928: My mother never had an affair with James Joyce. She did not unsuccessfully beg my Catholic father for a divorce which she knew he would never give. None of my brothers entered the service and I never at that time or any other received a letter from overseas.

1929: We were not in the sort of position to be affected by the Great Crash. Nonetheless I made no effort whatsoever to enter college. I couldn't carry a tune. I was not keeping a diary. I certainly did not spend that fall in Milan.

1930: Nothing happened.

1931: I was not asked to contribute to any periodicals. I didn't die. I belonged to no group in particular. I had never heard of Dada and was unacquainted with any of its participants.

1932: Though the thought of starting a family was by no means abhorrent to me, it seemed that it just never entered my mind. I didn't meet with a near fatal accident while out horseback riding with an olive-skinned distant relative.

1840:   I wasn't born. I was not blessed with prophetic dreams.

1933:   I didn't realize at that time the great potential that I was wasting. A nervous breakdown did not occur to me just then nor did I suffer from unpredictable seizures. I was not a virgin.

1934:   I wasn't near Paris and I have never seen Australia, Rome, Germany or the Azores. The house did not catch on fire that spring and no one was injured. That Thanksgiving was not a sparse one. I was not asked to stand up at the wedding of a close friend who was marrying very much against his will, nor did I get into a fight over a misunderstanding of the nature of my origins (i.e., insinuation of illegitimacy).

1935:   My mother never had an affair with James Joyce. She did not unsuccessfully beg my Catholic father for a divorce which she knew he would never give. None of my brothers entered the service and I never at that time or any other received a letter from overseas. I was not authoritarian. I was not working for an accounting firm on 78th Street.

1300:   I did not die by drowning. I was no judge of character at all.

1936:   I was not considered an orphan. I didn't drink heavily and never smoked.

1937:   I didn't begin what turned out to be a lifelong friendshp with John Frieder. I wasn't shy, envious, impatient, persistent, self-assertive, gentle, tired or bold. I didn't give large parties which tended to grow out of control.

1938:   I did not arrive home late for dinner one night to find all my possessions out on the street and a father dead set on disinheriting me. I never had any money. I never bought shoes in Florsheim's. I never objected to anything that anyone did.

1:   I never saw Christ nor visited Venice. I wasn't bitten by my own Irish setter.

II.

1925:   I was not born to a robust gypsy mother and a tubercular father.

1926:   I did not suffer from colic. Nor was I the victim of amnesia.

1927:   I did not beg my mother to leave a light on in the hall. I did not notice my genitals. I did not leave my food untouched at all.

1928:   I was not able to read or speak Latin having never heard of Mozart or Locke. I did not succumb to diptheria and spend six months in an oxygen tent.

1929:   I didn't break my arm.

1930:   I planted no bulbs at all that year.

III.

1930:   I didn't make preparations to pass through the birth canal.

1931:   I found no appendages on me. I was not seen lying on the lawn.

1932:   Unable as yet to speak, I did not know what to say or do. I did not want to be a fireman.

1933:   I was spared the horror of an early death.

1934:   I wasn't walking. I couldn't see or hear. I had no idea.

1935:   l was not molested by a retarded nephew. I was not a comfort to my bereft mother.

IV.

1934:   I was not born in July in a sunny hospital on Long Island overlooking the ocean.

1935:   I was not brought to a hospital for an emergency operation on a tiny ill-formed liver.

1936:   I was not making funny little sketches with a box of pastels which turned out to be poisonous and consequently my mother did not wrap me up in her coat and I was not given a special antidote which produced a drunken sensation.

1936:   *1945:*   *1962:*   *1294:*   *1738:*   *1873:*   *1937:*   *1034:*   *1555:*
None of these dates pertain to me.

Motion
(Basis of Position)

If insensibility grows turgid, though nothing decays, is rooted or up-rooted, nonetheless motion allowable in this instance makes traces just as milk does when it is mixed with water. This shouldn't be permissible according to logic which in turn should not be possessed before existence, but then, who says so? I should not feel the rubbing, the scraping, the indifferent staining. I should not have said before that I had felt something passing. But think of it that just before feeling becomes possible, there is the flashing sensation of a space (jar, box, can?) opening in every possible division of direction. There is also something that has never been thought of as opening. The possibility of my being has passed through every conceivable motion though I have no memory of any of them. If I had the modicum of intelligence concurrent with existence, I could perhaps explain this better; but I do not have the cluster of fuzz which elicits this nor am I close enough to the magnetic cloud to have anything or to want to be understood.

Feeling

Here lies the beginning of the confusion. The feeling before feeling is. Something is not able to be spilled. A mark in the floes marks the flow. The wooden splinter curls up with the appropriated reflexes of the cat. The nature of the blank is attractive beyond comprehension. Perception from a great distance sends sparklers which are no use at all. On this occasion the basting does not secure the taste for it turns out that nothing is cooking. Are you colder (kinder, tougher, broader, closer?) than you are? And have I been feeling more or less nothing? Nothing feels confused. Enough?

Nothing is as weighty as it seems. *Non-existence* appropriates the speckled area of *nothing.* The shade of difference between these terms (things?) is a shadow which thickens, the first appearance of sensation, the standard of measurement for the concept of a degree of feeling. (For example: Non-existence = N.E. Nothing = N. Then N.E. + (-?) N. = S (shade of difference; also standard measurement). Now "Anger" = A but to record its intensity we might say: A1S, A2S, A3S, and so on, until A10S, which might employ murder as part of its expression).

Feeling blank is feeling _____. To begin feeling I would attach _____ to _____. Wrapped with _____ this might produce _____. The first direction this would move in would be _____. It would travel along _____ for _____. And it could then be expressed in conversation as _____ _____or _____. To sustain it I would _____. To stop feeling that way I might _____ after _____ _____.

Position, Motion and Feeling

Nearly pointless guesses which will be and perhaps should be ignored by organisms which I do not resemble... Could it be said that not moving up or down, I am neither anxious nor calm. Having nothing to move and nothing to keep still... But to step aside from nowhere, to retard nothing permits motion to appear by way of a guess as the split-second visible creator of one vast bas-relief after another. This position might fit into as well as be analogous to the moment between the striking of a match and the vision of the flame. Bas-relief. Since it is extraordinarily difficult to twist non-existence into this deeply impossible position, the turn thus effected is usually less than 1 degree and the depth of field (its possibility of extension is directly proportional to the angle of removal) becomes greatly reduced. Oddly enough (enough?), this precarious and inaccurate position (the only barely possible one for that which isn't?) allows for the feeling of motion which further precipitates a brief brush with feeling. For example, at .043 degrees was I feeling what is called peaceful when being tucked in and out of a diagonal line of dust? Was it anger to have been collecting more and more of what I was being made to whip back and forth in? Was it sorrow to be floating in a substance which caused peeling and then splitting? Was it joy to be twisted by chance .000000016 degrees further by a tiny bubble? At .07 degrees is the motion of a smooth landing akin to love at first sight? Is pain an electrical storm? At .123, when bombarded at random by a particle shaped as "I", was I that "I"-conscious? Is the manner of reasoning which is spread through this section inherent to the intelligence, coincidental with the logic toward which "I" am aiming, or am "I" aiming these guesses back almost into nothing far from where those tiny, assymetric targets could be understanding?

Nothing Ends

The twist bends away. Surely, I have spent no time. In the unbended non-moment, I find nothing preventing me from speaking. Fewer and fewer bullets of "I" fly by. Surely, I have spent no time. I have nothing to go by. Soon I will not catch "I" on the fly. Know the fairly great assimilated poet to have said:

> He disappears before he appears to disappear still. His bound-less energy is his only boundary and it isn't his. Do not look for his footprints in the sand; rather, look at the sand and see it form a bountiful laugh. The distance or disparity between what is seen and what is imagined will, at the middle point, give or lead to his position which is not his.

Here lies the next to the last sentence which is coincidental with a slow braking, a release, a bombardment and dispersion. I...the last sentence is perhaps the most difficult of all.

Triplication:	'Plic' And 'Tion' Fall Heavily-With Continued Usage May Cause Large Amounts Of Lip Tissue To be Worn Off Self-Assertive
Trisection:	Movement (Or Evidence Of) Based On Itself And The Above Two
Quadruplication:	Found In The Stomach Cells Of Colorful Invertebrates Used In The Treatment of Sanity Soulful and Doleful Not Unrelated To Four
Five:	FFFFF IIIII VVVVV EEEEE
Six:	
Seven:	There Are Seven Words In This Sentence.
Eight:	There Is One More Than Eight Words In This.
Nine:	
Ten:	This Sentence May Be Divided And Re-United Into Ten Words.
Fraction:	Ryth _____
Zero:	A (O?!) Baited Breath A Line

Multitude: Summer
Winter
Spring
Fall

Fewness: Winter

Repetition: Summer

Infinity: Fall?

Form:	Pockets And Their Inversions:
Amorphism:	A Series Of Miniature Punches
	(Based On) Long And Short
Symmetry:	Non-Fictions And Fictions
Distortion:	Dependent On: Containers, Clamps, Threaded
	Lines: Trembling Corners (As Though
Angularity:	Stuffed Tightly With Hundreds of Shell-Less
Curvature:	Clams Pushed In Three Directions With A
	Force Equal To That Applied By The
Straightness:	Clam Itself To Pull Its Shell (In Other
Circularity:	Circumstances) Closed;
	Remaindered Suctions, As In A
Convolution:	Willow Breaking;
Rotundity:	Scarred Motion;
	Abrupted Vision;
Convexity:	A Jinx, Granular Seduction;
Concavity:	Prototypes; Accepted Channel;
	What Turns Out: Capable of Relaxation;
Flatness:	The Thought Of Taping Together;
Sharpness:	Whatever Can Be Settled On;
Bluntness:	
Notch:	
Fold:	
Furrow:	Opening: Closure: Perforator: Stopper:

Motion: Eccentric Form Of Lateral Melting
A Heading Toward And Its Trail Or Its Mirror
    Image
Basis Of All Fatal Diseases
Flying Within Weighted Outlines
Inserter

Study for Further Definition of Motion:

(Each time the most pertinent motions will be those which will become most apparent in the inverted state; in the turning of the book around to bring these movements upright, let motion be defined; the special theory of relativity (position of observer relative to motion) continues to pertain):

quiescenceimpulserecoilaccelerationpropulsion
tractionhauldepartureinsertionextractionleaprotation
oscillationagitationsurgepivollibrationunutation
trochilicperforateinterpenetrated.

Intellect:	'Odor' of Significance
	Double-Jointed
	Spice Plant
	Stage Manager
	Squat

Wrapped In A Hair Shirt (With The Idea of String Pulled Tight Around It) Made To Jump Over Itself!

Combine Fictions To Make This Non-Fiction!

| Absence of Intellect: | As In the Moon's Blue Ear |

Thought:	Sheaths of Pressurized Steps (Sometimes Graduated)
	June
	Roman Columns of Untouched Half-Air
	"I Have A Thought" Is A Thought About The Possession Of A Thought By A Thought In A Thought.
	Not Itself
	Turkey

Can Go Either Way!

Incogitancy:	The Hesitancy of Some Opaqueness To Evaporate Often Brought On Just By The Noise of Vacuum Cleaners
	Consider: A Bathrobe In A Pocket Or A Skull;
	A Door As A Fly Only More So;
	Based On The Loose And Tight Bases (Again?) For What Is Underneath

Idea: Growing
        A Nickel
        Salvaged Extremities

        Peek!

Topic: A Pattern of Consistency/The Consistency of
            Patterns
        Misshapen (?) Vectors
        Antithetical Necklaces

Answer: A Mixture (Compound) To Be Found Within
            Degrees Of Deviation Made Apparent By Such
            As:
                Never Stop Opening The Same Vise!
                Move Twelve Spots Through Three
                    Dampnesses!
                Make Time Out Of Wax!
                Use Only Water's Twin!

            To Be Arrived At Through A System To
                Change The Nature of Systems!

Experiment: Dilation of Fibers Into Non-*Non*-Lenses
             Wet Pointing
             Stepping Off (And On?)
             Cyprinodont
             Humour
             What Enters The Pencil, As Lead Leaves It
             That Which Is Between 'Divers' and 'Diverse'
             Any Perceiving
             All Thoughts

Comparison:	For Definition: (1) 'Clear' (2) 'Hazy' (3) 'Unclear' (4) 'Gone'
Discrimination:	'Hazy' To 'Clear'
Indiscrimination:	'Hazy' Through 'Gone'
Measurement:	Employs Any Arrangement Of The "Comparison Group"
Evidence:	'Clear' About 'Gone', Any Degree of, Even Not 'Gone'
Counter-Evidence:	'Hazy' To 'Unclear' (Or 'Unclear' to 'Hazy'!)
Qualifications:	Measurement (Using All Comparisons — See Above) Further Comparison. Some: Partially 'Clear'; Slightly 'Hazy'; Nearly 'Gone'; Almost 'Unclear':
Curiosity:	

A Virtual Hole And As Yet Unheard Of Refinement
  Of A Radio Wave
Used in Conjunction with *Sidereal* Muscle Which
  Sucks Itself Pink and Turns About (Inside Out)
May Use Dense Lemon Wings

Sew This Into Plastic — Use As Replacement for
  Appendix!

Incuriosity:	Curiosity With A Cold Or In Profile
	Incuriosity Something Something!
Attention:	Usher
	Non-Demolition Site
	First Degree
	A Circuitous Route Which Appears Straight?
	Completely Abstracted Coke or Pepsi
	Lining
	A Race Without Fingers Near One With Them
	Do
	All That Remains To Be Paid To Caesar
Inattention:	Crumpled Attention
Care:	Compressive-Effusive Mechanics
	Knitted Landscapes
	Scud
	Release of Sap Into Pockets (Breasts?) Or Onto
	Implied Circumferences Of Moving
	Solicitation Of Temperature To Seasons
Neglect:	Blue Care
	Based On Such Thin Sheets Of Fire That They Feel
	Lukewarm
	Weaving Done With Lead Sinkers
Inquiry:	This Motion- ? Why Not? In Which Way Not?

Possibility:Impossibility:Probability:Improbability:Certainty:
Uncertainty:Reasoning:Intuition:Sophistry:Demonstration:Con-
Futation:Judgement:Misjudgement:Discover:Over-Estimation:
Under-Estimation:Belief:Unbelief:Doubt:Credulity:Incredulity:
Assent:Dissent:Knowledge:Ignorance:Scholar:Ignoramus:Truth:
Error:Maxim:Absurdity:Intelligence:Wisdom:Imbecility:Polly:
Sage:Fool:Sanity:Insanity:Madman:Memory:Oblivion:Expectation:
Inexpectation:Disappointment:Foresight:Prediction:Omen:Oracle:
Supposition:Imagination:Meaning:Unmeaningness:Intelligibility:
Unintelligibility:Equivocalness:

Collective Definition:

A.

Amalgamation of Suspicions and First Drafts
Mirror Sponge
Twisted and Ascending
Any Specimen, Any Craps
Daily Lifting of Occurrence
The Corrugated View
Just Before
The Lone Ranger
Indeterminate Basis of Its Opposite Through on
A Deeper Level Equal To It
Portrait of Wires Done In Fiction
Good or Bad Weather
Almost Retarded Energy
The Memory of the Removal of a Specific Quantity of 7-Up
Snaps

Or
B.

In Association With Legwork
Loading
Gravel Recording A Change of Pace

Helen Keller or Arakawa

A Selection

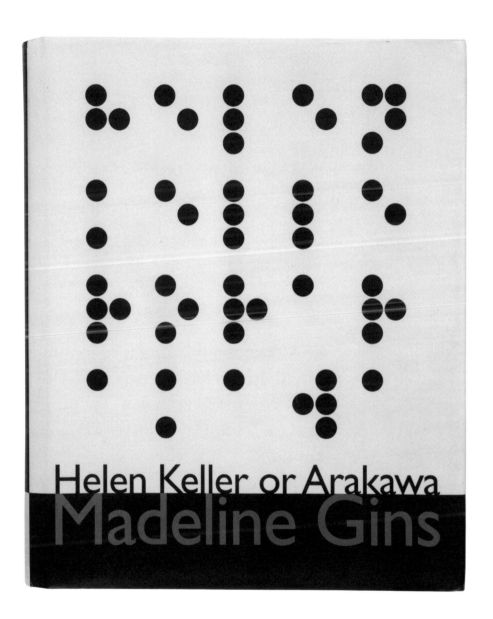

Helen Keller or Arakawa

Madeline Gins

CHAPTER I

Thinking Field

"The sum of it is that you are a blessing, and I'll kill anyone who says you are not."
—William James (in a letter to Helen Keller)

"The invisible and the imperceptible weigh not the same."
—Anonymous (deafblind)

The afternoon has much to recommend it, including an all-inclusive atmosphere with evening, and a geometry that's flexible enough.

I was definitely born on July 6, 1936, or it may have been June 27, 1880, or was it actually November 7, 1941?

Form rubs its antlers against trees of not much. If projective envelopings did not move persuasively, there would be no world. Sky of an I.

Helen Keller. The main constant not to be forgotten is that two of my senses are perpetually down: for seeing and hearing, I — and any I of this variety — draw a blank every single time.

Well, that's how it is and it couldn't have been otherwise save for a change in conditions so total as to have permitted me never to have been Helen Keller in the first place.

Only a totally other set of conditions could have made it possible for me not have to have been a Helen Keller.

Subjected to similar constraints others might live the self-same name, and, by generating sequences of events identical to those associated with this my name, come up with this sky of an I and no other.

Take, for example, this fine, sharp specimen of great odoriferous dimension, a freshly baked loaf of bread in front of me, and know it — the bulk of it and every crumb! — to be for me invisible. For you, too, I suppose, the bread is, at this instant, more or less invisible.

Indeed the whole range of my perceiving happens within what most people consider to be the invisible. "Invisible," is a term I've imported from the sighted world. It's but one of many tales told to me, into me, so that I might form — for the sake of my forming — as if I could — an abiding picture of the world. (The main supplier of certain of my impressions may be memory, ancient, for as an infant I had sight, retaining it until I was nineteen months of age.)

But, in fact, I find nothing I perceive to be essentially invisible. In a world of all blind people, everything would be non-visible, and it would be trivial to point out one thing or another as being so. To the blind, terms like "invisible" are but polite bridges (with much torque and of odd construction) to the sighted; curtsey, and say, yes, ma'am. When I'm not speaking in the other's voice, I perceive things directly, fielding them as best I can.

Nevertheless, a having once been marked with the condition of invisibility goes so far — so far-going has it been in this marked vessel as to have completely spread through me — as to lead to where it began: myself observing myself unseen. Here's the sum of all of that (and soundless!), plus a whole other set of x's, hidden. As the provisional sum of all of these, I direct the traffic of weightedly perceptible "invisibles" from a within. The nearly perceptible is thoroughly perceptible enough to me. I have never been able to find the cut-off points for this within. Rather, this "within" acts as if it were boundlessly stretching out — if one were to include the full spread of all the ripples and ripplings — into a distance ambiguously endless.

Weight Without Place (1980-81).

Of course, actions taken by me have a great deal to do with how this distance forms. More than fifty regular actions and easily the same number of micro-actions determine enveloping and the *tissues of density* near and far on which this depends.

And this is the way I do inhabit the non-visible; as a stretched-out mass onto which the layout of the world is to be placed to be remembered. The "living canvas" is not a bad nickname for someone who strives to keep track of things the way I do. Distinct spots tell of themselves proprioceptively or kinaesthetically. What's happening within my right shoulder is two and one-quarter feet distant from what goes on within the left one. The "living canvas" forms as the distance between spots. One moment's spot is another moment's distance. I situate things and events by means of these. Spots, areas, distances expand and reduce to become one another, occasionally without my knowing it. I have what's happening within my left shoulder *cleaving* slightly less than two and one-quarter feet distant from those events peculiar to my right one.

A Man Walking (1968). Walking or Talking (1969). Determining Body (1987-88).

I keep these two shoulders separate and at the distance from each other that they, by nature, by the nature of (my) body, deserve to be; only when I'm forced to move exceedingly fast — to go as swift as a bullet — do I allow them to be given as a single dot of a place named shoulder.

Then let Helen Keller be simply s/he in whom the world draws kinaesthetically its grand home around and about and precisely wherever.

The universe (my intimate as much as yours, but inasmuch as I never catch sight of the many possible separations which, I am told, are constantly presenting themselves to you, then, perhaps my intimate even more so?) exacts a universe of consequences. Were this any less exacting, I'd be strangled by a compromised exactitude. Here's a case in which less *is* considerably less.

I'm told that (but do I need to be told that?) pivotal points get seen from three vantage points: eye level, looked up to, glanced down on. Around the meat of point, and out from it, tentatives assemble and are drawn as lines. The triad of elemental paired opposites of orientational space (front-rear; above-below; left-right) runs aground or doesn't. The background laps up the background. The possessive of the moment binds the fixation.

Elementary Atmospheres (no. 2) (1974-75).

The canvas is divided up from each single point of view severally. Likewise "who" parcels himself or herself out as the concept of person comes alive at the nexus of all (its) tendencies and tentatives. At which juncture, the sky of an I might scratch its head.

To draw the retentive network from an array of attentivity remembered, depicted. Actions can be passed through these lines. There's a graphic abeyance — held in graphic abeyance — and there's a graphic obedience, a continually transitional conferring. This is the linear stuff of the transitive. Of the what of there. Enough of this and perception will have conferred upon the world a sense of its having been seen — and that happens transitively.

Afternoon and Evening (1974).

It can be said that, because it falls everywhere, the phenomenon of light is all-transitive. With perceiving, it is much the same. Even the slightest registering of anything at all equals an alighting on something and to alight on something counts as the direct hit required for a being transitive onto something. Springing into action and everywhere being sprung into action, perception bombards the world as itself, hitting into itself transitively.

Or Air (1973-74).

In a world of the all-transitive, a world composed of a medium passing (passing? — sieving) through itself (itself? — its set of events), actions associated with intransitive verbs ("the bird flies"; "he runs") can be thought of as, left and right, scoring numerous direct hits within themselves (within themselves? — within the flying; within the running) and so as supporting a full transitivity. I am thinking of what manages to have carry-over onto what.

What in line draws itself along and through as line if not the perceiving of it? Some of the gaze narrows to a stare then heads into and combines with the firmly drawn line all down its thin but ample length. Lines that hold the narrowed-down stare within the gaze are sometimes seen as, and from time to time are spoken of as, themselves staring out. Usually straight lines are the ones that appear to be staring, but even curvilinear lines can be firm enough and sufficiently straight to be seen as staring out from the surface.

The impressions must be kept distinct, apart from one another, to keep their distance, they suggest. Even so, they must live in the steady stream of the waterfall of their textures collecting. They have a forward and a back. They have an odor off to the side and straight behind. The nub of position is rife, and if respected, it signals. It is a graphicality, kinaesthetic and tactual, that is sketched in by me, at me, every single day. If the visual finds me, it is through my kinaesthetic graphicalness that it does. Kinaesthetic graphicality.

It's the neutral presentation of the thinking field itself (its group of activities) that I — and I — seek here. In each case, I proceed to search out the rallying points of alignment. I begin not as one isolated dot in a field but as a dispersion of these throughout body.

In the substratum of the visible lies a foundational graphism, full quick of thick, of some size but *sizeless*, brought on by any accumulation of sentience, marked out in all directions and practically knowing this by definition. No matter what, it is the *sizeless* that is giving the measure to events, that's why it's all so difficult. The *sizeless* fits an edgeless contour. So named, "it" stands with the non-sized but as a something named — named, *sizeless*, of course; even so this is a term that would deny all objecthood — for objects come in sizes. Similarly, to the *sizeless*, all possibility of being abstracted must be denied — for to be abstracted from one form to another would require at least initial allegiance to one size in particular.

The ethos of the *sizeless*? The *sizeless* moves us and is of us; even as this is of us, what would the *sizeless* have of us? Who is it who is without size but would speak, rather? And how many *sizeless* skies of an I within one *sizeless* sky of an I? These swoop up and scope, non-calibratively, through what I speak of as *atmospheric resemblances,* temporarily building *moral volumes* out of those (more than a little self-contradictory) spins that (doubly) *cleave.*

Although order of mention might suggest order of appearance in this limited page-by-page format, what is happening on the designated surfaces might be happening all at once. The shifting of attention happens continually upon the same plane, and through others. There is a locating. There is a locating of this locating. A continuous overall reading, involving a constant search for the possibly missed points of alignment.

Sufficient knowing of relational positionings and the consequent presentation of oneself to oneself as one blank screen (each screen is readily dissolvable into mere indeterminate area) after another are dependent on those sets of points or of tensions that must and do exist in order for there to be the relatively steady state of a continual non-collapsing all in upon oneself I direct the order of the scale of events, groups diminished past vanishing points, and cellular units grouped so as to be larger than might ordinarily be suspected. In saying this, do I assert too much? In which is found the chat of circumstances. It is forthrightly plasticity that willows, putters or purrs or thinks out and about.

I get up and walk around the giant banyan tree, and I walk around its circumference of about a hundred feet. No one knows how old it is. The size of the branches in every direction and the tremendous roots I scramble over give me the impression of a grove, but what it is is one colossal tree. I know for certain it is not a part of my face, I think.

CHAPTER II

"Perception Has Got to Have a Body!"

I f the thinking field of the deafblind person were absolutely dissimilar to that of his or her fellow, s/he would have no means of imagining what they think.

A network for retaining possible alignments might come about with the writing of this. They key term would be *to cleave*, taken simultaneously as "to adhere" and "to [be] cut apart." In order for something to be able to be thought of, or for an object to be perceived, something (some event) will need to be adhered to, no matter how briefly; and coupled with this, for the sake of other thoughts or perceptions to come, so that there can exist the characteristic condition of receptivity, there will have to be a cutting apart from this to which there had been the need to adhere.

Throughout my body as one longish heart I know the destiny of human society will be to live turned inside out with all consequences on the table. Those sequences making up any observing are to become themselves observable. Observable events are potentially reproducible ones; eventually, from these sequences a whole new perceiver or a new other might be generated.

Within gravity, within inertia, within the cell, the synapse, the ambiguity, biological and otherwise, I hunt (and so must s/he) for, among other specificities, *that which cleaves within the cleft*, so that we might, for example, yes, learn to live to be our own posterity!

On the subject of voice, all these questions were put to me at once: "Where does it feel as though your voice is coming from? As this is arising in you does this feel as though it were coming from not one place but many? And what in the world would be the qualitative feel of this to you . . . would you try to say?"

Voice is a ball that only collects into the being of one in the course of something's being said — a ball made up of nothing but its own rolling out. Or voice is a precipitate. Or is this a chain of precipitates of . . . the whole of my movement? I make it out to be a precipitate that is practically a "photographic" report of mindbody. Voice comes — from head to foot — out the fingers of the right hand, with a lot of talk hanging around the wrist and a light march of it down through the whole length of the middle of the forearm; but lately I have tried to connect this to that pitifully under-used apparatus, my voice box.

For me, to force some sound out into the regular voice-world is a sorry affair. Where to aim? I have but the remotest idea of where to aim, I have no means of checking up on myself in this. Still this remains one dimension I'd like to be able to pull out of myself.

How do I move? I can move only by eating up or dissolving where I am. I (anyone) pull in with a bright gulp what is to come next. When walking forward, I also snake along on three parallel, horizontal planes. I cast standpoints and send out runners or tendrils of what I call *forming spacetime*. Following this, projective circumferencings happen with me at every level, and *on all or any scale*. All with quirks of their own. Everywhere proceeds as its own tame whirlwind as *then but spreaded blind perception quirks continually sudden*. All these squirmings and divings add up to what spacetime is. What is spacetime?

With the bending and exploding of frameworks, forms of self-preservation suggest themselves. Some shapes hold things apart. I, the maker of these shapes, am subjected to, and must act in accordance with, proddings from near and far as to what to name them. Then a shape takes to tunneling through body, and that shape, along the entire long length it takes for and as itself, shivers and sits to be as open as a mouth in roaring laughter. Sometimes hidden down far along within this lengthening of a designated volume, I glimpse a small pile of nearly twigs; no hand can reach this.

In perceiving lies the telling (into someone) of stories a'composing — as in "compose yourself" — writ in sand, dust, particles, waves, and in all and any sweep of thick of quick, dire or not. Of course dire.

What if seeing and its basis could be separated? Most people would think that not possible. For them, nothing could be more counter-intuitive. I'm reminded of that chart made up of but a single dot that was even so identified as "two or three dots [that were] unable to be separated." Might there be an underlying basis for seeing, and, if so, would this be detachable from the actual seeing of things? What I understand (and work with) as the basis of seeing consists of mindbody in its apportioning of itself and the rest of the world out into a thoroughly proprioceptive-kinaesthetic (and tactile) graphicality.

It is in the nature of the thinking field to move and instigate behavior using points of position and of supposition. Here is a world of complete tentativity.

I myself am supporting evidence for the ultimate separability of seeing and its basis. This yields, submerged and compact, an accommodating layer, one come out of extension, stretched over itself. This —

from one discrete end of it out to the other — serves both as the primary instance of distance and the means by which all other distances will then be measured, envisaged.

I can keep a dot marked "head" apart from that marked "foot." It is out across upon the "living canvas" that these stay separate. Knowing these discretenesses and their locales to be the stretched-out bases (blank receiving areas) for seeing... something's taking place upon these bit by bit.... I sometimes wish for the construction of a great new visual organ whose interior would be a spherical handball court with a mark-leaving ball that, bouncing everywhere I'd need it to, would turn any spot it touched into something I'd be seeing. The ball *cleaves* to the wall, then bouncing back off it is *cleaved* apart from it (the wall) only then to be made to head for yet a new spot for *cleaving*. The ball in this image is hardly a ball at all, or one only provisionally, always more of an amassing than a mass. If *cleaving* could amass in place — and I think it can — why, it would be just the "ball" for this.

What is *cleaving* or what is it to *cleave*? What may be thought to be sandwiched between the two senses of "to *cleave*" (to join and to be separated) is the "material" of thought itself, conventionally held to be "transparent" or "transparency itself." A medium that is a perceiving texture may be said to be formed within and between the occurrent juxtaposings of the two contradictory actions of to *cleave*. This medium is the sum of the actions composing it; the result of all *cleaving* that, as it takes place, has formed and is forming whatever is in the offing. The habit of referring to this medium as "transparent" causes it to be erroneously thought of, even if only ever so slightly, as an object rather than as the set of actions which it is. After all, there exists the expectation, indeed slight, that whatever is transparent will at least have to it, if nothing else, a front and a back; but, just as when it comes to the ocean, which is also hardly merely an object, we find no readily locatable front or back, there is neither simply a front nor simply a back to the perceiving texture or the medium that constitutes thought. If the ocean as a whole cannot be spoken of as being transparent neither should the perceiving process be. "Action constructing itself as 'see-through'" might

A Man Walking (1968).

be a better way to refer to the characteristic "transparency" of thought. Although people may guess that it is by means of *cleaving* that they think and perceive, they cannot directly perceive this to be so. Even so, I'm told, the process, carried out in the see-through mode, manages to bring about a world that has to it various degrees of opacity. Some opaque objects will be shiny.

Put the world of numbers along one line (horizontal), and the world of things, names of things, along a line running parallel to this (where are these — wherever could these be?), and together let these show how seeing might always be put. An apparatus for recording "who" in action. This starkly has the look to it of not more than enough. It sets as it rises within that spectrum extending from the hue that is the memory of lead as marked to the color of saliva as it is being swallowed in shyness or boldness. This unit made of two horizontals crosses the length of the canvas, straddling a rectangle that occupies the top two-thirds of the surface. Below "squats" a rectangle that's of distinctly different proportions from the painting, but of which it is nonetheless stated: *This rectangle is a photograph of this entire painting.* Note that as difficult as it is to produce an image on command, it is an even more difficult task, perhaps an impossible one, to "see" a photograph into (or out of) a blank. What's more, the frame within which the called-for photograph would have to materialize is, as noted above, not of the right proportions and so of little help. Could the viewer produce at will photographically into this long, low box a visual record, matte or glossy, of what, in the wider context of the canvas as a whole, s/he sees the entire painting (isolated rectangle included) to be? Or does this empty rectangle "represent" an over-exposed photograph — one that has come out blank — and nothing more. Or, inasmuch as the wrongly-proportioned rectangle gives more than a little disjunctive pause to the act of ascribing, could it be that, more than an image of any this or that, this is a "photograph" of, or the possibility of a photograph of, "OR" itself, pivotally nude. Or do the edges of this photograph that doesn't look like one provide flat report of a hypothetical proprioceptive-kinaesthetic graphic substratum to the visual? — and as such, then, are this rectangle's drawn edges representative of the walls (skin) of that self-apportioning out creature known as observer?

Separated Continuums (1964).

The forms I harken to are schemas of what might be there (and will be again) and of what has happened to me. They are pictures of schemas of pictures. I break my head against the images that don't form every time.

To be transitive is to have a carry-over onto something else. Thinking, I find, works as a field that is all transitive. So thought commands a body all spread out in transitivity.

"The best way to draw a line is to do it with your eyes closed!"

"I now declare myself to be carrying that over onto this."

It was with the help of two carefully condensed and separated out thick lines or *separated continuums*, that I was able to know when I had entered Green Park. Roughly, one line to fix things and events occurring all along my path at levels from mid-thigh to ground and the other running line for noting events happening at levels from the shoulders on up. What happened in between was sorted out and shared by these two dominant projected continuums. I smelled grass and burning leaves. It was a blessed corner in which to commune with nature away from the street traffic — men, women and children walking for the pleasure of it, dogs gambolling without leash or muzzle, pigeons and gulls. I touched the noble plane-trees and oaks, and enjoyed the softness of the grass. The sparrows were very cocky and so fearless we almost stepped on them. We inquired why the plane leaves were being burned, and the reply was that it takes them five years to rot. Their ashes make a fine dressing for the soil.

"Perception has got to have a body!" I cried.

CHAPTER III

The First
Little Brick
of Substance

No point or dot can be of the size conventionally accorded to it. This is because there can be no such thing as an uncontained point. The perceiving of a point or dot amounts to nothing less than a containing of it. Therefore, when it comes to approximating total point size, size and scope of the origination container, that is, perceiver and the world, must be added onto the designated *minimum visible* that is the point seen. Even so, the point (with dot in tow) continues to be that which is commonly put forward as being the small-est of all objects or notations.

No point exists such that it is non-living.

"I am *almost individual.* How can all of voice have made itself this small? That down towards which everything, when reducing, must go, that is I. The limit of a reducing down towards. Beginning with the usual fluffery of reference, trim in to have self-diminished to dot, drawing ever-tighteningly towards less. And you would find this to be pancake flat. Smallest-sized, in that state of. And even in this minuteness, still I can clear my throat. Then down further, at this small size, sphericality and rectilinearity notably blend: my squared corners are round. And still I am not vanished. Due to ever-present drift or blur, I am, in some ways, never 'small enough.' This adds up to 'small enough': no longer any smaller-still toward which to advance by subtraction or by concentration. The ceasing of all or any tending towards, for the position has been filled. Finally, the desperate need to be brought even further down in scale may be relinquished — and something sits back in an easy chair."

On a vertical canvas, a bottomless entity appears as a container of grid and not much more; the subdividings — geometrical cellules — of this grid that encloses itself into a containing form (of, to begin with, itself) grow smaller when approaching what the title tells us will be the bottomless below. This is a wide this, wide-what-open, wide open at both ends or endlessnesses. Whatever this is, it is procedural and linguistic. What is stringing itself out here, then remaining put, is evidence of the forming and the containing of a container in the making, the unfolding and the subsisting of deductive events of a thinking field. A dot on the lower right is labeled "mother." This would be the point of departure for, or what stands in for, all of what is mother for the while. This dot as marked stands for a greater contextual whole and not only for someone's mother, perhaps the artist's, but for the one to whome this thought or memory occurs or for a motherly point or site in a particular sky of an I.

Bottomless/ Mother (1961).

"A psychological double bottom is declared in the antiphrastically entitled series *Bottomless*, where the arrows and diagrams accompanying the stereometric 'object' as it passes through various vicissitudes, clearly show that the process of geometric conversion and reduction is to be read as the narration of a psychic trajectory," one of the early reviewers wrote.

"After a while I went very near to a beautiful white rose-bush which was completely covered with buds and sparkling with dewdrops; I bent down over one of the branches with a lovely pure white bud upon it, and kissed it softly many times; just then I felt two loving arms steal gently around me, and loving lips kissing my eyelids, my cheeks, and my mouth, until I began to think it was raining kisses; and at last I opened my eyes to see what it all meant, and found it was my precious mother — that expanding dot — who was bending over me, trying to kiss me awake. Do you like my daydream? If you do, perhaps I will dream again for you some time" — written when I was eight years old.

It is important to know that each dot stands definitively for something — except when it doesn't — and to know exactly for what it stands and to agree to a name for it. This is what begins the traction on the world: the pinning down of one thing, anything. Not only must the world be cleaved into sections, agreement must be reached as to how these various sections are to be named. If one thing is not stopped, stopped in its tracks, no traction can be gotten on the world, on oneself.

Before I had caught on to what language was, and to the arbitrary and voracious centrality of its game — I got this all in one shot — I wasn't even able to. . . . Nothing had been marked for the rest to pass by for. If even one demarcation can be made (at knowing), the rest, assembling itself accordingly, follows.

I had to learn — and it was a question of agreeing to a convention — a method of affixing to each thing the realization that this indeed was the thing that it was.

This is what people do: they let "x equals dot "stand for "y equals mother." A dot x might stand for a thing y.

He was the sum of his dots, as marked, that group of stand-ins for living points. We saw him walking or talking.

"But the customs officials didn't see him, at least not right away. They wouldn't allow the work in 'duty-free' if it was only printed matter and not art. A few dots could be anything, for any purpose, but if these were of something, then it would be art and there'd be no duty. 'Look at the title,' I said. 'You see it is called *A Man Walking*. Here are dots marked head, thorax, pelvis, hand, leg and so on. See how the dots marked arms and hands have been placed a little higher up than where they would normally be expected to be? This is because as the man walks along his arms are naturally swinging back and forth as part of the gait.' 'Oh yes,' they said, 'one foot is quite a bit in front of the other, too. You're right, someone is walking across the dark blue . . . .' 'Grid,' I supplied the missing word. Everybody got quite excited by this new, very reduced chart — a few of the customs men were actually jumping up and down. Although it had the semiotic ring to it of its own period, the sixties, this anatomical chart of another order could have stood for any person of any time out for a walk, from homunculus on up, a strolling Neanderthal, an ambling Midlothian, a disjunctive grouping of post-modern humanoid jumping beans."

A chart with a life of its own. In subsequent versions, each bit of pinned down abstraction, each named dot, gets assigned a dual stand-in role. The dot linked by arrow to the designation, "head," is now, by means of a second arrow, also given over to the word, "sky." "Thorax" and "mountain" make do with one dot between them. Parts of the landscape are paired with parts of the body, generally according to the corresponding positions held all up and down that vertical that is the human figure when it is standing outdoors. The semantic doubling, however, cannot be said to follow this predictable path. Instead, a dot associated with a small, black stenciled-in presentation of the word "leg" gets paired with another "leg," also in stencil letters, but in this case large, light-gray ones. Has the same denotation been given twice so that we might not miss that this is really what it is? Or are we being clued in to the need to view the chart in relation to different image sizes. Or do we have in this the report of a seeing and then a seeing again, a matter-of-fact routine occurrence, smacking, even so, of deadpan double take?

The dot for "foot" as well as doubling as a mark for "shoe" ("shoe" is larger in size but much paler than that "foot" with which it shares a dot and which supposedly wears it) is allied, a third arrow lets us see, with an indefinite something that's hardly a word and possibly never to become one. What started as a chart of a man out for a walk has now become and will now bear the title of *A Study of Twins (Talking or Walking) (1968)*.

This artist makes "specific abstractions." Without the existence of a specific and critical abstractionism, the present study would not have been possible.

The extreme transitivity of that waiting texture which is the thinking field, for all its colorful motion into the world of any texture, is of unrecognizable temperature, unlike either the body of the observer or of anything that is being observed.

"It is all a blanket thermometer and one wonders whether it will ever succeed in taking its own temperature."

Then let's rethink all this in terms of Voluntar, in terms of her story. Voluntar, short for voluntary action, is herself the archetypal degree. An elusive warmth. In the scale of events, she, preceding dot, is beneath it yet wider. When she collects in place, she can manage to work herself up into being point or dot. Once set in motion, these two images (dot and Voluntar) cannot help but bleed into one another. It is said that the movements of her wisp of body configure animate microchips that are volition.

Voluntar is a great little diver; I should know for it is I who trained or invented her. It is she who takes motility and builds it into mobility.

Voluntary activity, earned rather than given, is a result of or a lithe product of an historico-cultural development in behavior, and as such is considered to be a feature unique to human psychology. The capacity for voluntary activity distinguishes child from beast. "I'd rather like to do that." Yet the child is capable of far fewer voluntary actions than is the adult. Lack of training curtails range and amplitude of choice. This is dependent on the number and types of dives made by Voluntar. Her broadening the horizon as one spasm of the horizon after another builds the world. As the first little brick of substance, she is the ultimate fibre of a micro-ground. I may have seen photographs, or, if you like, "photographs," of these twists and twistings.

Ceaseless expeditions might describe the extent of her effort, her way of life, the relentlessness of it. Not all microscopics dive so well or as often. She pseudopods below, looking for all the world like an octopus, could only she be seen.

It's not that she sees for me, for she's as blind as I am. What she does is feel the way for me. She is a blind man's cane, but a soft, small, internal one, with *a core of flexibility only*.

Voluntar, then, is substance and sign (structure) of the voluntary. We have in her the signpost (many) leading humans to a specific scaffolding of behavior that breaks away from biological environment to new forms of culturally-based processes. As down Voluntar dives and up again each time she comes with one *signified or if* after another, a sky of an I is sketched out and the basic unit of "who" is constructed.

She is countless yet there may not be as many of her as that would make it seem. She is also free not to exist.

It's at the backbone-crossroads of her hinge-nature that I pick up the *call of continuity* each time. Her sleek body is slinkily prescient.

Or take her momentarily in the static state of having agreed to be point or dot. She is the always figurative point. All concrete figurative. Only through voluntary action can she be summoned or do the summoning.

Found lounging in the figurative, sword in hand (or pseudopod-like projection as sword), suddenly she lunges forward. Upon her having lunged forward, all swords vanish except for their points. When the sword's point strikes, that's her it becomes. *Point* has been her pseudonym for centuries.

Voluntar goes directly from zero speed to top speed. Intensity is her middle name, actually. Her knowing how to spring into action without missing a beat allows her to catapult on a regular basis to the forefront of issues. Marx greatly admired how swiftly, surreptitiously, and definitively she could be effective; he wisely chooses to rely on her as key mover in a central dictum, declaring: "We have sufficiently explained the world, the *point* is to transform it." Without her, it couldn't be done, and if not by her, then by nobody. Anything Voluntar does is transformatory in full, and this will include anything whatsoever that has been transformed.

I know her to be the darling of place markers of plasticity, limning character and will. *Stretchable impressions* are yes, her, hers.

It was not long before lines were being drawn. None of these had any less firm a resolve of plasticity throughout than did Voluntar.

The body of a dot is drawn out and given traction to be pressed into line. Voluntar's speech is one with that of dots telling how it feels to be drawn out into line. Unwillingly pressed into service? That's unclear. If we cannot know what they think and feel, how can we ever stop discriminating against the miniscules. We may not care much for how it feels to go from point to line, but for them this is major. We think of bodies as being all different sizes, but mindbody we would reserve mainly for ourselves, that is, for beings who are our size. It's easy for us to do this as long as the little others remain voiceless. But these can speak if only we listen. They speak in us, to be sure, but when they would speak up, directing their attention to their own unique subject matter, it turns out that for these partials, these littles, only a smattering of English is available; rather, Voluntar and her peers can avail themselves mainly of Anglo-Saxon with now and then a little Sanskrit mixed in: "It all came rud, pud as a thud, that is. Pud extrud. They scud. Curded line or line-like turned cud. [Sounds that are made within the inscribing of a line] Cud of what? Sense cud but. Anu [Sanskrit:atom] then. Trodded. Cud rudder. Suds as duds. Sudden. A bud of paddhati [line]. Bud bite, oh! Bud in Buddy. O Bud. . . . Light budding. Cram bud into pud. Rub bud of pud into the crevice of line. Pud creamier linear. Huddles. The hum in the pud. Charcoal puddles. Line active."

sources

It is in the nature of this book to be a "sharing of nameless," one that passes through the words and images of Helen Keller and Arakawa and others. Even so, the written sources should be listed and here they are:

Most, but not all, of the poems that are part of this work are composite texts: *The Mountain to the Pine*, which is part of chapter xvi, contains a great deal of Rimbaud's *Marine*, several lines of *The Mountain to the Pine* by Clarence Hill, a blind poet friend of Helen Keller, a haiku by lkkyu, and more than a little of *Maker Between Above and Below* by Arakawa and Madeline Gins; in *Short List: The Agnostic Mountain Speaks* one of the few lines that has been carried over from the original *The Mountain to the Pine* to the composite one is reworded and redirected. *Great Poem*, belonging to chapter xvii, is signed Z. M. for Zen Masters and these are Heishin, lkkyu, Kakua. In chapter xix, there is a fragment of a Paul Celan poem, the second stanza of Helen Keller's *Niagara*, a poem by Dogen (this appears again with further explanation in chapter xxiv), and two fragments from poems by the Zen masters Koseisoku, Sogyo, and Ejo. *To and From Plenum* in chapter xxiv takes its tone and many of its words directly from the Nietzsche poem *Bird Verdict*; it makes use of several lines from Stacy Doris's *Virus*, and the declaration central to and embedded in Mallarmé's *Un coup de dés*. The *Middleground* of chapter xxvii is a Reverdy poem, *Inn*, but presented only in part and combined with a question that Arakawa asked in his paintings in the seventies.

Chapter vi pits the diction of Kakuzo Okakura (*The Book of Tea* and *Ideals of the East*) against that of Helen Keller. A section from Denis Diderot's *D'Alembert's Dream* also has a role in this.

Chapters vii through xi, as well as chapter xii, and chapters xvii through xix have extended throughout them a very tampered with version of practically the entire fourth chapter, "Space," of John Buchan's *The Moon Endureth*; in various of these chapters material from André

Maurois's *The Weigher of Souls* is mixed in as well.

Passages from Marius von Senden's *Space and Sight* appear in chapters iv and xvi.

Chapter xix has within it a short section from von Kleist's *On the Puppet Theatre.*

Paragraphs have been taken from the writings of Max Born (*The Restless Universe*) [chapter vii]; René Char (*The First Moments—* tr. M. A. Caws) [chapter v]; Robert Creeley (*Some Place Enormously Moveable*) [chapter viii]; Mario Diacono (*Arakawa: A Quadri-dimensional Geometry of Imagination*) [chapter iii]; Frederick Engel (*Revolution in Science*) [chapter viii]; Charles Haxthausen (*Looking at Arakawa* and *On Blank Dots*) [chapters ix and x]; Marc Le Bot (*The Blank Chaos of Arakawa*) [chapter xiii]; Mark Lindner (*Contingency and Circumstance in Architecture: Venturi and Scott Brown's Sainsbury Wing*) [chapter xxv]; Jean-François Lyotard (*Longitude 180—*tr. M. A. Caws and *Que Peindre*) [chapters iv and xxii]; Abraham Pais (*Subtle is the Lord*) [chapter vii]; William Prescott (*The Conquest of Peru*) [chapter xvi]; Cecile Rossant (*Hidden Text*) [chapter xiii]; Gershom Scholem (*Kabbalah*) [chapter iv]; Leo Steinberg (*Other Criteria*) [chapter xix]; and Emanuel Swedenborg (*The Infinite and the Final Cause of Creation*) [chapter x]; and Mark Taylor (*Saving Art*) [chapter xxv].

The initials associated with the texts at the end of chapter xxii stand for: Francis Ponge, Kakuzo Okakura, Helen Keller, George Rodenback, and Janet Bloom.

—M. G.

index to titles of Arakawa's works*

*Editor's note: The index has been changed from the original publication to reflect only the titles that appear in the *Madeline Gins Reader* and the pages they appear on here.

Editor's Acknowledgments

This book would not be possible without the support and permissions kindly granted by the Reversible Destiny Foundation. Many thanks to Stephen Hepworth, Momoyo Homma, Peter Katz, ST Luk, Amara Magloughlin, and Miwako Tezuka for the knowledge they have shared as well as for their unstinting encouragement and assistance. Archivists Kathryn Dennett and Elizabeth Noe were also crucial to the book's formation, and scholar Jondi Keane's research into Arakawa and Gins's archive was as illuminating as he is gracious (i.e., very). Andrew Durbin, Tess Edmonson, Michael Slosek, and Irene Sunwoo, at *frieze*, *Canadian Art*, the Poetry Foundation, and Columbia University's Graduate School of Architecture, Planning and Preservation, respectively, offered platforms for writing and speaking about Gins's work at significant moments in the development of my introduction. Charles Bernstein, Mary Ann Caws, Amelia Schonbek, and Hayley Silverman generously imparted their insights into Gins's life. Readers Thomas Beard, Shiv Kotecha, Tan Lin, Susan Stewart, and Rachel Valinsky provided invaluable observations as I attempted to arrive at a final version of the introduction. Thanks, too, to Matthew Shen Goodman and other colleagues at *Triple Canopy* for their interest in Reversible Destiny and amazing work in general. Lastly, it is to the extraordinary dedication and skillful eyes and hands of Lisa Pearson that the object you hold in your own hands (and behold with your own eyes) owes its existence; my warmest thanks and admiration to her for the one-woman masterpiece and world-restoring project that is Siglio.

—LI